hotels • restaurants • resorts • spas • shops

malaysiachic

For regular updates on our special offers, register at

www.thechiccollection.com

hotels • restaurants • resorts • spas • shops

malaysiachic

text lucien de guise • fay khoo • gabrielle low • mathew maavak •
curtis marsh • elena nichols • kerry o'neill

thechiccollection

editor
valerie ho

assistant editors
priscilla chua • janice ruth de belen • josephine pang

designers
annie teo • felicia wong • wong hean meng

production manager
sin kam cheong

sales and marketing director
antoine monod

sales and marketing managers
rohana ariffin • suresh sekaran • chris kok thian chai

first published 2008 by
editions didier millet pte ltd
121 telok ayer street, #03-01
singapore 068590
telephone : +65.6324 9260
facsimile : +65.6324 9261
email   : edm@edmbooks.com.sg
website   : www.edmbooks.com

©2008 editions didier millet pte ltd

Printed in Singapore.

isbn: 978-981-4217-13-2

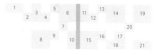

cover captions:

1, 14, 15 AND 16: *Four Seasons Resort Langkawi.*

2: *The bar at Tamarind Springs.*

3: *Rhu Bar serves tropical cocktails in a Middle Eastern setting.*

4: *A traditional wayang kulit (shadow puppet) performance.*

5: *A traditional kite, known locally as wau.*

6: *The Spa Village lap pool at the Pangkor Laut Resort.*

7: *Traditional Malay instruments.*

8: *A woman snorkelling in Sipadan off the east coast of Sabah.*

9: *A male hornbill carrying prey.*

10: *The Petronas Twin Towers at night.*

11: *A view of the sunset in Langkawi.*

12: *Rejuvenating floral baths are available at The Villas at Sunway Resort Hotel + Spa.*

13: *Royal Selangor is renowned for its pewter products, including jewellery.*

17: *The Rafflesia flower is the largest flower in the world.*

18: *A deluxe suite at the Casa del Mar.*

19: *Thai cuisine is served at Poppy Garden.*

20: *@mosphere Modern Dining is the place to go to enjoy some of the finest food and best views in Malaysian Borneo.*

21: *The luxurious interior of one of the villas at the Kudat Riviera.*

THIS PAGE: *A Malaysian appetiser made with glutinous rice and ikan bilis.*

OPPOSITE: *The pool at the Tanjung Jara resort.*

PAGE 2: *One of the cosy suites at The Villa in Kuala Lumpur.*

PAGE 6: *A school of pomfret near a shipwreck site in Malaysian waters.*

PAGE 8 AND 9: *The great outdoors is never too far away regardless of where one is in Malaysia.*

contents

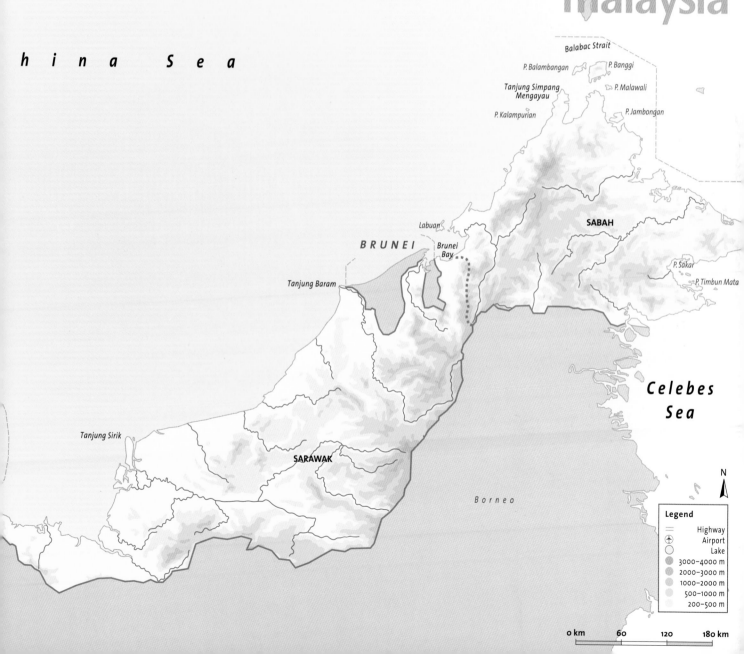

PHILIPPINES

Sulu Sea

malaysia

hina Sea

Balabac Strait

P. Balambangan

P. Banggi

Tanjung Simpang
Mengayau

P. Malawali

P. Kalampurian

P. Jambongan

SABAH

Labuan

BRUNEI

Brunei
Bay

P. Sakar

Tanjung Baram

P. Timbun Mata

*Celebes
Sea*

Tanjung Sirik

SARAWAK

N

Borneo

Legend
Highway
⊕ Airport
◯ Lake
3000–4000 m
2000–3000 m
1000–2000 m
500–1000 m
200–500 m

0 km   60   120   180 km

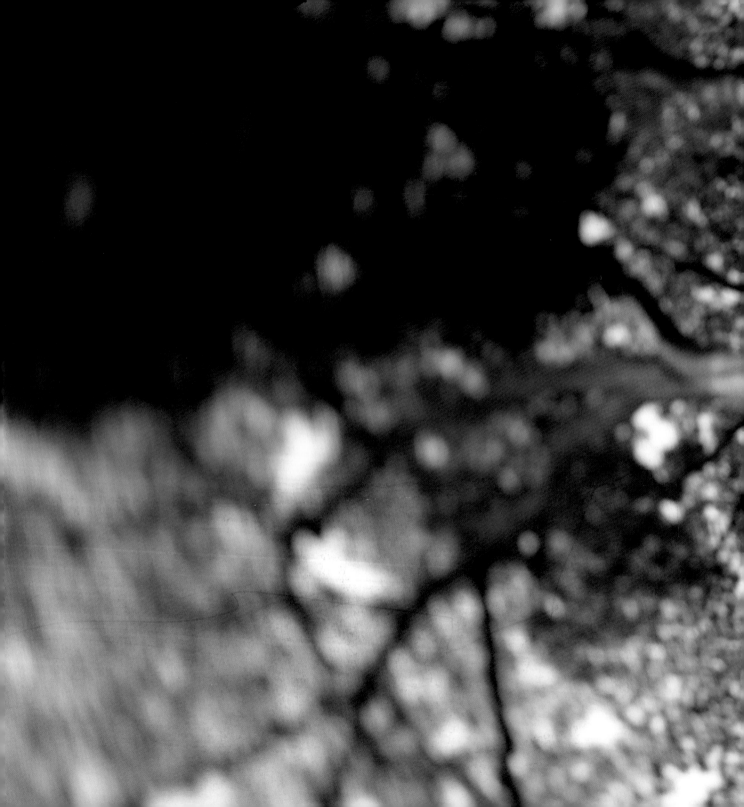

introduction

blessed with nature's bounty

Malaysia has been promoted in many ways over the years—'Fascinating' and 'Truly Asia' are some of the more recent slogans. Both of these are accurate, but there is more. Above all, this is a country blessed by nature. There are no earthquakes, typhoons or volcanoes; seasonal flooding is the only blot on the landscape.

Natural beauty is all around. From rugged rainforest trails to some of the world's most elegant resorts, there are many refuges from the rat race. This is possible when the land area is a third larger than the UK while the population is only 27 million. Modern and yet largely unspoilt, it appeals to visitors as diverse as the late Luciano Pavarotti and the tireless Joan Collins. The rainforests are among the oldest in the world and the beaches are fringed with palm trees. The East Coast state of Terengganu has some of the most spectacular resorts, including Tanjong Jara and the Aryani. The best underwater activity tends to be a more rugged experience, mostly located in East Malaysia dive sites such as Sipadan Island. On land, padi fields glow with a vivid green that brings out instant sentimentality among urban Malaysians.

In Malaysia's more rural locations, little has changed since the tropical-paradise standard was set by the island of Tioman in the 1958 musical *South Pacific*. Even the capital city has its visual high points. The Petronas Twin Towers were until recently the world's tallest buildings and have appeared in numerous feature films as well as being visited by the Aga Khan when he gave the building an award. The towers are not only tall but also beautiful, filled with the discreet Islamic symbolism that is found throughout modern Malaysia. So attached has the nation become to this highly visible symbol that questions were asked in parliament when Sean Connery's *Entrapment* featured an unflattering juxtaposition between the two shiny skyscrapers and a slum with what might be a river or an open sewer.

The heart of Malaysia remains rustic, unchanged in some ways since the time when Conrad and Somerset Maugham evoked the land's tropical lushness. In a nation whose economy depends much on agriculture and industries, there is still plenty of nature to go round.

all for one

Malaysia is also blessed by Man. Racial diversity is among the most valuable touristic assets of this one-stop tour of Asia. Three of the continent's great cultures are represented: Chinese, Indian and the indigenous Malay. The Chinese and Indians tend to hang on

THIS PAGE (FROM TOP): Snorkelling is a favoured sport in Malaysian waters, such as Sipadan off the east coast of Sabah; the Black and Gold Birdwing butterfly can be spotted at the KL Butterfly Park.
OPPOSITE: Danum Valley in Sabah is one of the primary rain-forests of Malaysia.

more tenaciously to their ethnic customs than their original homeland cousins. The home grown Baba-Nyonya mixture of Chinese and Malay culture is well known. The population is growing, but not quite at the rapid rate envisaged by former Prime Minister Mahathir Mohamad, who was aiming for 70 million Malaysians by the year 2020. The major cities continue to expand. Kuala Lumpur is by far the biggest metropolis and is as much a magnet for so-called 'outstation' locals as for foreign visitors. This city is where Malaysia's sometimes sleepy image is least valid. It is as vibrant as any city in Asia, with a little less traffic chaos than some.

The majority of Malaysians are more traditional than the urbanites of Kuala Lumpur—universally known as 'KL' by a nation that loves to abbreviate place names. It is a young city with an exploding population. This includes a large number of overseas-educated professionals who have brought back with them an international approach to life that includes living away from home and staying up late. At one time the government tried to impose a curfew to keep family values alive as married men were spending too much time enjoying KL's nightlife. The city now caters to almost every lifestyle and lower income earners are not excluded from the action as hawker stalls are often at their busiest in the early hours of the morning.

Unlike many parts of Asia, Malaysia does not have an obvious disparity between the rich and poor. Instead, tycoons and government leaders flaunt their enthusiasm for the same roadside eateries that are favoured by the man in the street.

Being a country with links to almost every part of the world, Malaysia has been welcoming visitors, tourists and expatriates for many centuries. Big spenders are more welcome, and there are conspicuously fewer backpackers to be seen here than in most parts of Southeast Asia.

At the top end of society is a unique arrangement of royalty. Malaysia is divided into 13 states, of which nine have royal families. Of these, the Kedah sultans can with some seriousness trace their lineage back more than a thousand years. There used to be one more 'royal house', perhaps the most unusual that Asia has ever produced. The English family that produced generations of 'White Rajahs' of Sarawak was dispossessed in 1946. This state and its neighbour, Sabah, are located on the island of Borneo, separated from Peninsular Malaysia by a large expanse of ocean. In many ways they are separated by rather more than the South China Sea. With so many royal families in Malaysia there is considerable interaction

THIS PAGE (FROM TOP): Iban boys playing in a river in Sarawak; a view from the 88-storey, 452-m- (1482.9-ft-) tall Petronas Towers across the city of Kuala Lumpur.

OPPOSITE (FROM LEFT): Street hawkers selling one of the local delights—satay (meat on bamboo skewers); view down the centre of an illuminated bridge in Putrajaya.

between the hereditary elite and the rest of the population. There is an unusually complicated and thriving honours system which bestows awards to citizens and sometimes to resident foreigners such as Ferrari boss Jean Todt, whose Malaysian celebrity friend Michelle Yeoh is also a 'Datuk', a title similar to a British knighthood that is conferred by the heads of the various states. At the social summit is a system of kingship that offers another unique Malaysianism—the seat rotates among the nine sultans every five years.

culture + consumerism

Visitors to Malaysia are not usually motivated by the quest for cultural monuments. Little has survived from more than a few centuries ago. It is the living history and heritage of the different races that makes the country so exceptional. Malaysia's past has always been tied to trade, and the Strait of Malacca remains one of the world's busiest mercantile route. Today, Malaysia continues its commercial links with every continent.

Rather than being filled with museums and art galleries, the emphasis is on skilled crafts. Although it is not a nation of fashion victims, all the big brands are present. Social life revolves around shopping malls that are sometimes more impressive than anything found in the West. Leather boots and jackets work better in air-conditioned shops than on the tropical streets outside. The urbanites' way of life seems to be a constant movement between homes, chilled offices, restaurants and, of course, luxury cars. Although the vehicles are expensive, this is still a cheap place to have a driver.

At the same time Malaysia has successfully clung to its regional identity. Much of the more recent fashion looks back to colourful cultural roots. Batik is one of the buzzwords in the world of local couture. The revival was given a boost by the late wife of Malaysia's Prime Minister, Dato' Seri Abdullah Badawi, whose efforts even made an impression overseas. Meanwhile, those Malaysians who have made their way in the world are just as welcome back home, as national heroes. The best known of all, thanks partly to *Sex and the City*, is Jimmy Choo.

In keeping with the country's steady acquisition of international glamour is a sophisticated concert hall for the Malaysian Philharmonic, with well-known guest conductors such as Carl Davis making regular appearances. There are also the attractions of Formula One racing, which brings the sports-loving global glitterati to town. Probably the most potent symbol of progressive Malaysia is just outside KL. Genting Highlands was once known for nothing more than Malaysia's only casino. The gambling remains but the hill resort is positioning itself as the Las Vegas of the region, bringing in big-ticket entertainment.

THIS PAGE (FROM TOP): Michelle Yeoh, an international celebrity is involved in charitable work with both foreign and local communities; Batik has become a symbol of national pride and the national dress for formal occasions.

OPPOSITE: A busy crew at a refuelling pit stop during a Formula One Malaysian Grand Prix.

PAGE 18: The majestic Mount Kinabalu in Sabah.

...attractions of Formula One racing, which brings the sports-loving global glitterati to town.

architecture

The Petronas Twin Towers may be Malaysia's most defining landmark, but the country's architectural landscape is a more complex fabric; a mirror of the numerous identities and aspirations that constitute the nation.

kuala lumpur

Kuala Lumpur is a tropical metropolis, an Asian boom town, a sprawling and uneven patchwork of shophouses, kampung houses and colonial-era civic buildings interspersed with monumental building projects, office towers and rows and stacks of mass housing. It is a landscape that is first world, and third, and changing.

Now around 150 years old, the city, often known as KL, has never had a single, dominant architectural identity. Even in its early days as a trading post, there were distinguishable differences in how the various communities constructed their wood-and-thatch dwellings.

The British, who came in 1880, transposed the architectural style of one colony to another. Borrowing from India's Mughal architecture—the pavilions, arches and onion domes—they built the **Sultan Abdul Samad Building** (Jalan Raja), **Kuala Lumpur Railway Station** (Jalan Sultan Hishamuddin), **Railway Administration Building** (Jalan Sultan Hishamuddin), Town Hall, now the **Panggung Bandaraya** (Sultan Abdul Samad Building, Jalan Raja), and other government offices, as well as **Masjid Jamek** (Jalan Tun Perak). Only the **Royal Selangor Club** (The Padang) was constructed in a mock Tudor style reminiscent of home.

A new, flamboyant crop of buildings emerged with the rise of tin, rubber and revenue farming magnates. Mansions and villas were a showy composite of Italian arcades, neo-Classical columns, Victorian embellishments and Chinese feng shui principles. Among these, the **Loke Mansion** (273A Jalan Medan Tuanku) is still extant.

The shophouses so characteristic of the Straits were, likewise, dressed up with Western-style façades. Decorative features ranged from neo-Classical to baroque carnivals of floral tiles and plaster-moulded swags. The decorative style of choice in the 1930s was Art Deco, which can be seen not just on shophouses but also on other prominent structures, most notably the **Odeon Cinema** (Jalan Tuanku Abdul Rahman), **Central Market** (Lot 3.01 & 3.07, 1st floor, Central Market Annexe, Jalan Hang Kasturi), **Oriental Building** (Jalan Tun Perak/Jala Melaka), Anglo-Oriental Building, now **Wisma Ekran** (16 Jalan Tangsi), and **Rubber Research Institute of Malaya** (260 Jalan Ampang).

The International style, which gained a foothold here after World War II, is exemplified in **Federal House** (Jalan Sultan Hishamuddin), **Chin Woo Stadium** (Jalan Hang Jebat), **Harrisons & Crosfield** (70 Jalan Ampang) and the **Loke Yew Building** (4 Jalan Mahkamah Persekutuan).

As the capital of the newly independent nation, the nationalist fervour and post-colonial identity crisis of the period following Merdeka prompted attempts at articulating what would constitute a

Malayan, and later Malaysian, architectural idiom. KL had, and still has, the responsibility of bearing the symbols of statehood. The earliest responses tended to be literal, with vernacular architectural elements, such as kampung house roofs, grafted onto large-scale institutional buildings like the **National Museum** (Jalan Damansara) and **Parliament House** (Jalan Parlimen).

Adaptations of vernacular Malay and Islamic architecture continued to be seen in the following decades in state showpieces such as the **National Library** (Perpustakaan Negara Malaysia, 232 Jalan Tun Razak) and National Theatre, also known as **Istana Budaya**

(Jalan Tun Razak) and, to greater effect, in the **National Mosque** (Jalan Sultan Hishamuddin) and the **Dayabumi Complex** (Jalan Sultan Hishamuddin).

At the same time, however, individual architects were driven by their own concerns. Hijjas Kasturi introduced a sculptural eloquence to the KL skyline—**Tabung Haji** (201 Jalan Tun Razak) with its slender contours, and Menara Telekom, now **Menara TM** (Jalan Pantai Bahru), with its elegant asymmetry, prefigured by **Menara Maybank** (100 Jalan Tun Perak).

For others, a regional architectural idiom rises naturally out of responses to local climatic conditions. Ken Yeang, in particular,

architecture

pioneered high-rise buildings adapted to the tropics with buildings such as **Menara Mesiniaga** (SS 16 Subang Jaya, Selangor). Yet another approach to the question of identity lies in the use of indigenous materials and building methods. Constructed by master carpenter Ibrahim Adam and based on a design by architect Jimmy Lim, **Rudinara** (Sungei Merab, Bangi, Selangor) is an outstanding example of a dialogue between traditional and contemporary architecture.

Beginning in the 1990s, architecture was seen not just as a medium through which to mirror the identity of a nation, but as one that would shape that identity. National pride and aspirations were expressed with fist-in-the-air bravado in mega-projects like the **Kuala Lumpur International Airport** (64000 KLIA, Selangor), **Kuala Lumpur Tower** (2 Jalan Punchak off Jalan P Ramlee) also known as the KL Tower, and, most famously, the **Petronas Twin Towers** (Kuala Lumpur City Centre), designed by the American architect César Pelli.

In a period that saw the proliferation of numerous mega-projects, Putrajaya was perhaps the largest and most ambitious. The founding of a city on an oil palm estate created for architects what was in effect a blank 4,931-hectare (12,185-acre) canvas. Every single aspect of the new city was planned and designed from scratch, including an artificial lake, the requisite commemorative monuments and futuristic street furniture to complement the look of the surrounding buildings.

In tandem with the with Malaysia's push for new national symbols, or perhaps as a result of it, a greater emphasis has been placed in recent years on the conservation and adaptive re-use of pre-existing structures. In KL, recent examples include **Wei-Ling Gallery** (8 Jalan Scott, Brickfields), where the interior of an old shophouse has been transformed into an art gallery by a network of walkways which maximises the space for exhibiting artwork. Another example of re-using architecture is seen in the **KL Performing Arts Centre** (Sentul Park, Jalan Strachan), built around the original brick structure of an old railway workshop.

Throughout all this, the question of identity never left the discourse. If anything, it has become more complex. And to a large extent, this has been reflected in the work of younger Malaysian architects. Earlier preoccupations with climatic solutions have now been given a greater urgency by contemporary global concerns about the environment, energy conservation and material use. At the same time, adaptations of vernacular architecture have become more subliminal, seen more in spatial configuration rather than in symbolic references. The most recent, significant examples of such architecture have primarily been smaller-scale structures, such as the minimalist **67 Tempinis** (67 Jalan Tempinis Satu, Lucky Garden, Bangsar) and the innovative **Safari Roof House** (463 Jalan 17/13A, Petaling Jaya, Selangor).

west malaysia

Throughout the country, the distinct character of each place is reflected in its architecture. Melaka's hybrid architectural identity is most evident in its historic core, where a Portuguese church, Nossa Senhora da Anunciada, also known as **St Paul's Church** (Bukit St Paul), looms over what was once a **Dutch administrative building** (Stadthuys, Town Square, Jalan Kota), a Victorian fountain and a clock tower built by one of the town's leading Chinese merchants. Other landmarks located in Melaka include the **Cheng Hoon Teng** (25 Jalan To'kong), the oldest Chinese temple in Malaysia, dating back to the mid-17th century, and **St Peter's Church** (Jalan Bendahara), the country's oldest functioning Catholic Church, built in 1710.

George Town's former glory as a cosmopolitan trading post can still be discerned in structures like the **Eastern & Oriental Hotel** (10 Lebuh Farquhar), a grand 19th-century hotel once owned by four Armenian brothers, **Masjid Kapitan Keling** (Jalan Masjid Kapitan Keling), an imposing Indian-Muslim mosque, and **Khoo Kongsi** (18 Cannon Square), a sprawling clan complex centred around a magnificently ornate clanhouse. All of these have been carefully restored, as have smaller-scale buildings such as the **Penang Heritage Trust office** (26A Stewart Lane) and **No. 3 Love Lane**. Another model of restoration is the **Cheong Fatt Tze Mansion** (14 Leith Street), a 38-room Chinese courtyard mansion that has been converted into a boutique hotel.

architecture

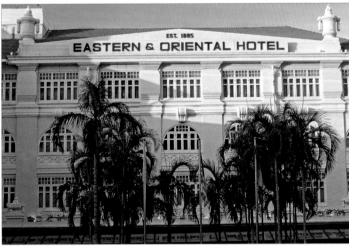

George Town is also home to a number of neo-Classical buildings constructed by the British for their colonial bureaucracy. Among them are the **Town Hall** (Jalan Padang Kota Lama) and **State Assembly Buildings** (Light Street). Similar structures can be found in the former tin-mining towns of Ipoh and Taiping. These include the **City Hall** (Jalan Kelab, Ipoh, Perak) as well as the **Perak Museum** (Jalan Taming Sari, Taiping, Perak) and the **Larut Matang and Selama District Office** (Taiping, Perak).

Spread out in between West Malaysia's towns and cities are rural settlements, or kampung, where the traditional Malay house is the most prevalent architectural form. Regional differences have given rise to variant forms—the Johor Malay house, for instance, tends to have a prominent polygonal bay with full-height shutters, while houses in the east coast have tiered roofs with curved ends that bear a closer resemblance to Thai and Cambodian vernacular forms. Traditional wooden houses, however, are rapidly being replaced by generic concrete structures.

Mosques are another distinctive building type throughout this region. Among the most notable are **Masjid Ubudiah** (Bukit Chandan) in Kuala Kangsar, Perak and **Masjid Zahir** (Jalan Pekan Melayu) in Alor Star, Kedah, both of which were built by the British in the Mughal style.

While these mosques exemplify an imported architectural style, there are still a number of mosques that embody the Southeast Asian mosque typology, characterised, among other things, by tiered,

THIS PAGE (FROM TOP): The Leong San Tong clanhouse, located at the heart of the extensive Khoo Kongsi clan complex, was completed in 1906. The decorative work was executed by master craftsmen from the southern region of China's Fujian province; touted as 'The Premier Hotel East of Suez', the Eastern & Oriental Hotel's past guests include Noel Coward, Hermann Hesse, Rudyard Kipling and W. Somerset Maugham.

OPPOSITE: Masjid Ubudiah in Perak's royal capital, Kuala Kangsar. Designed by the British architect Arthur Bennison Hubback, it was officially opened in 1917.

pyramidal roofs instead of domed roofs. The oldest surviving mosque of this type is **Masjid Kampung Laut** (Nilam Puri) in Kota Bharu, Kelantan. The same roof form appears in a number of mosques in Melaka, including the 18th-century **Masjid Tengkera** (Jalan Tengkera, Melaka).

The varying features of the physical terrain and the availability of relatively undeveloped swaths of land throughout West Malaysia have recently led to a number of important contemporary works. These include **Sekeping Serendah** (67 Jalan Tempinis Satu, Lucky Garden, Bangsar) in Serendah, Selangor, the **Boh Visitor Centre** (Sungei Palas Tea Garden, Jalan Gunung Brinchang, Brinchang, Cameron Highlands) in Pahang and, most recently, the **Universiti Teknologi Petronas** (Bandar Seri Iskandar, Tronoh) in Perak, which revisits campus architecture within the tropical context.

east malaysia

Longhouses are perhaps Borneo's most distinct architectural form, and an integral part of the identity of communities like the Iban and Orang Ulu in Sarawak and the Murut and Rungus in Sabah. These communal dwellings have traditionally been built of timber, raised on stilts and sited along rivers. In general, longhouses comprise private family apartments and a common area, usually a verandah or gallery, which is shared by the entire community.

Some communities, however, have eschewed traditional building materials like timber, bamboo and

architecture

thatch in favour of modern construction materials. Recent variations of the longhouse have incorporated concrete, fluted columns and pastel-coloured paint, while maintaining the traditional layout.

Other distinctive indigenous forms in East Malaysia include the Melanau tall house and the circular Bidayuh baruk (a gathering place for the community), which has spawned numerous contemporary adaptations.

Beyond vernacular structures, the most significant buildings are concentrated in the state capitals, Kuching and Kota Kinabalu. Under the regime of Charles Brooke, the second white rajah of Sarawak, Kuching was transformed into a colonial town with a series of government buildings modelled after European villas, castles and country homes. Among these are the **Astana** and **Fort Margherita** (both located on the north bank of the Sarawak River), the recently restored **Court House complex** (Main Bazaar, Jalan Tun Abang Haji Openg) and the **Sarawak Museum** (Jalan Tun Abang Haji Openg).

Located half an hour from Kota Kinabalu and situated amidst a verdant environment, **Sinurambi** (88812 Kota Kinabalu, Sabah) is one of the most exciting examples of contemporary architecture in East Malaysia. The structure is organically integrated with its surroundings through the use of local timber and stone quarried from the site on which the building stands, and through the use of extensive glazing and open decks to create a sense of permeability between the building and its environment.

THIS PAGE (FROM TOP): *Interior of the Sarawak Museum. The original wing, where this photograph was taken, was completed in 1891; the restoration of the Court House complex in Kuching has been widely acclaimed. The building dates from 1874 and now houses the Sarawak Tourism Complex.*

OPPOSITE: *The Astana was built as the residence of Sarawak's second white rajah, Charles Brooke. Completed in 1870, it currently serves as the official residence of the Governor of Sarawak.*

visual arts + crafts

While modern art mirrors all that is in flux in Malaysian society, crafts reflect the continuity of ideas, beliefs and practices in all of the country's diverse cultures. In general, Malaysia's contemporary visual art scene has, since Independence, been largely based in and around KL, while craftmaking can be found in towns and villages throughout the rest of the country.

kuala lumpur

Modern art in Malaysia is less than a hundred years old. The emergence of KL as a centre for artistic activity and discourse took place in the years following up to Independence in 1957, with the establishment of two art collectives. The multi-ethnic **Wednesday Art Group** was formed by British arts educator Peter Harris to encourage individual expression and experimentation, while **Angkatan Pelukis Semenanjung**, initiated by Indonesian-born Mohamad Hoessein Enas, trained Malay artists in the production of naturalistic, though somewhat romanticised, depictions of Malay rural life.

The post-Independence generation of artists were mostly foreign-educated. Returning from the UK, US and Europe, artists such as **Syed Ahmad Jamal** and **Latiff Mohidin** brought with them a preoccupation with Abstract Expressionism, adapted through the use of Asian symbols and images.

Reacting against the subjectivity and emotionality of expressionism, artists like **Redza Piyadasa** and

Suleiman Esa turned towards art-making that was more conceptual, more analytical and more reflexive. But the cold objectivity deployed by the self-anointed 'New Scene' artists, joined by Ismail Zain, was not simply a backlash against the dominant approach to art. By questioning the formalistic processes of art, they struck at the heart of the issue of identity. As they saw it, a Malaysian identity in art had to go deeper than the mere localisation of Western art forms, deeper than, say, the depiction of palm fronds in an Abstract Expressionist manner. It was form itself that had to be revisited. Postmodernism, wrote one commentator, had thus made its entry into Malaysian art.

The work of succeeding generations has tended to be more individualised, with many artists shifting their focus towards addressing social and political concerns. This is evident in the later work of Ismail Zain and Redza Piyadasa and in Nirmala Dutt Shanmughalingam's critiques on issues ranging from environmental degradation to the Vietnam War.

Among the artists who emerged in the 1990s, Wong Hoy Cheong has produced some of the most important and provocative work of his generation, dealing with issues such as migration, exploitation and colonisation. Other artists who have produced work with a strong social and political bent include Simryn Gill, Hasnul Jamal Saidon, Jegadeva Anurendra, Liew Kung Yu, Yee I-Lann, Nadiah Bamadhaj and Bayu Utomo Radjikin.

Signalling the end of the age of manifestos, artists that have emerged on the Malaysian art scene in the 21st century have continued to pursue their own individual agendas, and their work has been encouraged by the increasing number of galleries, private and government grants, residency programmes and the growing pool of serious art collectors who see the investment potential in art. Major galleries include Valentine Willie Fine Art (1st floor, 17 Jalan Telawi 3, Bangsar Baru) and Wei-Ling Gallery (8 Jalan Scott, Brickfields). A consistent highlight in the Malaysian art calendar is the annual exhibition at Rimbun Dahan (Km 27 Jalan Kuang, Selangor) which culminates its year-long residency programme.

west malaysia

Artistic expression in the rest of the Peninsula is alive in numerous craftmaking traditions. George Town, Penang is where dying trades seem to be making one last heroic stand. Among the crafts still produced by a handful of aging practitioners are handmade sandalwood joss sticks and incense cones, bamboo blinds, hand-engraved Chinese name plaques, Malay songkok, wooden chairs with hand-woven rattan seats and traditionally-worked gold jewellery (all of which are located in and around Lebuh Chulia). A little further afield are shops selling painted lanterns (42 Jalan Magazine), mahjong tiles and dice (45 Love Lane) and beaded shoes and sandals (177 Lebuh Muntri).

While mass-produced nyonya kebaya can be easily found throughout the country, Penang, one

THIS PAGE (FROM TOP): Bujang Berani, a sculpture by one of Malaysia's most important contemporary visual artists, Bayu Utomo Radjikin (metal and plaster of paris, height 100 cm (39 in), 1991); traditional Chinese lanterns hang over the main entrance of the Leong San Tong clan house.

OPPOSITE: A batik shawl trails behind a dancer at the 2007 Floral Parade in Putrajaya.

visual arts + crafts

THIS PAGE (FROM TOP, LEFT): Malaysian batik can be distinguished from Indonesian batik by its brighter colours and its more prominent crackle effect; Bangles from Sabah and Sarawak made with natural fibres; Malaysian Story No. 2 by key Malaysian artist and art critic Redza Piyadasa (mixed media, 1999); a craftswoman making a winnowing tray.

OPPOSITE (FROM TOP): A wooden mask produced by the Mah Meri of Pulau Carey, Selangor; an Iban man with traditional tattoos on his neck, shoulders, arms and legs, Sri Aman, Sarawak; a Kelantanese wayang kulit (shadow theatre) puppet.

of the centres of Straits Chinese culture, is perhaps one of the only places where kebaya are still embroidered using hand-guided machines. **Tai Kheng** (180–B Jalan Air Itam, Penang) is one of the longest running kebaya-making businesses in the country and counts among its clientele a 1960s Hong Kong screen siren and the wives of the local elite. **Kim Fashion** (170–4–77 Gurney Plaza and 33 Jalan Cantonment, Penang) also produces exquisite pieces and has a similarly impressive list of clients. A wide range of designs is available, from wide-eyed goldfish to children playing with firecrackers.

Pahang's woven silk, characterised by simple plaid designs rendered in rich colours, has only recently been getting the attention it is due. The newly styled **Royal Silk Road of Pahang** runs through four villages that specialise in silk weaving, although the centre in **Pulau Keladi** (Perniagaan Sutera Pulau Keladi, Bangunan Karyaneka, Kampung Budaya Pulau Keladi, Pekan, Pahang) has the distinction of having in the past catered exclusively to the Pahang court.

A more well-known textile form is songket, a type of brocade produced in Terengganu and Kelantan. **Pura Tanjung Sabtu** (5728 Kampung Tanjung Sabtu, Mukim Manir, Kuala Terengganu), run by a member of the Terengganu royal family, has one of the most highly regarded songket workshops around.

Other items produced in the northeast coast—known as the centre of traditional Malay crafts—include woodwork as well as kris and various traditional weapons.

Malaysian batik-making, adapted in the 1920s from Javanese batik production techniques, also originates here.

Unique to Terengganu is the production of brassware, while Kelantan has wayang kulit (shadow theatre) puppets, fine silverwork and wau, traditional Kelantanese kites.

Among the Orang Asli throughout the Peninsula, weaving with plant fibres is perhaps the most common form of craftmaking, primarily connected to making functional objects like mats, baskets and pouches. Despite their utilitarian purpose, the items produced are often embellished with motifs inspired by nature. The Semelai, in particular, are known for their intricately-patterned pandanus mats while the Jakun use complex weaving techniques to create areca nut containers.

The Mah Meri are known for their woodcarvings, which are rooted in the ritual use of wooden sculptures and masks. Other Orang Asli crafts include blowpipes, musical instruments, metalwork and ornamental objects like hair combs made of bamboo.

Recognising that indigenous craftmaking is a vanishing tradition, **Gerai OA** (www.coarc.org.my) is a mobile, non-profit group that works at developing and marketing crafts produced by indigenous communities. The organisation returns all sales proceeds to the communities.

east malaysia

Tattooing is a traditional artform in Borneo, linked to all aspects of the region that outsiders find fascinatingly exotic—headhunting, tribes and animistic beliefs.

However, not all of Borneo's ethnic groups have a tradition in tattooing. The most common are Iban and Orang Ulu tattoos.

Traditionally, tattoos were hand-tapped using bamboo needles and ink was made out of a mixture of soot, water and sugarcane juice. Motifs were often highly stylised zoomorphic images, such as scorpions and hornbills as well as composite creatures such as dragon-dogs (known as aso).

Some traditional tattoo artists were known to have rendered their services in return for payments of beads, pigs and parang (a type of machete), all of which were highly valued items. Most tattoos today are executed with modern equipment, although a few tattoo shops still offer hand-tapped tattoos.

The pua kumbu—a type of cloth that is tie-dyed before it is woven on a backstrap loom—is one of Borneo's most highly prized crafts.

An Iban craft form that is largely the domain of women, the cloths are regarded as spiritually potent. If the cloth depicts a certain animal figure, such as a snake, the animal must be 'fed' by weaving in representations of food.

Certain motifs, such as human figures, can only be woven by weavers of rank, and even then, only with the sanction of the spirit world. A master weaver is accorded a status similar to that of an Iban war leader, as the process of making a potent pua kumbu is likened to a spiritual battle.

Almost all of Sabah and Sarawak's communities have a tradition in working with plant material such as rattan, bamboo, tree bark and pandanus. As with the Orang Asli of the Peninsula, the items produced tend to be utilitarian, such as mats, baskets and housing material. However, plant material is also used to create personal adornments. The Bidayuh, for instance, have been known to use orchid vines to make woven bangles. Highly stylised motifs tend to be inspired by nature, myths and local scenes, and are often differentiated by ethnic group and village of origin.

Another major craft tradition in East Malaysia is woodcarving, associated with the production of items such as ritual masks and sculptures, shields, sword sheaths, charms, implements for weaving and tattooing as well as burial poles. Carvings are also produced out of material such as bone, boar tusk and horn. Also found in Borneo are weapons crafted from iron as well as brass, including musical instruments such as gongs, made by the Rungus, and ornaments such as brass earrings used by both Orang Ulu men and women to elongate their earlobes.

Borneo is also well-known for beads, made into ornaments or incorporated into traditional garments. In the past, beads were valued as a form of currency. They are still regarded as family heirlooms among many ethnic groups. These days, ceramic beads are still produced by the Lun Bawang, a community centred largely around Lawas in northern Sarawak. In Sabah, Rungus women produce beaded necklaces from seeds and fern stems.

bars, clubs + cafés

Nightlife in Kuala Lumpur has never been so good. Design-conscious bars nestle cheek-to-jowl with high voltage clubs and quaint cafés, catering to a gamut of tastes and predilections. If you're in Kuala Lumpur, there's absolutely no excuse for staying in.

kuala lumpur

It's hot in the city, and the hottest street *du jour* is the revitalised **Asian Heritage Row**. Jewels of this nightlife crown include **Bar SaVanh** (62–64 Asian Heritage Row), for Indo-Chinese cuisine and cocktails, and **Cynna House Lounge** (28–40 Asian Heritage Row), where the young and desirable boogie the night away over Grey Goose cocktails.

Around the corner, the freshly restored **Heritage Mansion** (Heritage Avenue, 18–26 Jalan Kamunting, Asian Heritage Row) is gaining repute as the nightspot of choice, with theme nights to further seduce punters. Further into the city, Bukit Ceylon continues to gain prominence with an ever-growing clutch of eateries and bars. **Frangipani Bar** (25 Changkat Bukit Bintang) has a fancy drinks menu that is complemented by the sleek patrons who frequent it.

Across the road, newcomer **Twenty One Kitchen + Bar** (20–1 Changkat Bukit Bintang) is frenetically fast-paced and boasts quirkily named cocktails and hip young deejays. Sophisticates will appreciate the finer pursuits of classical music and jazz at **No Black Tie** (7 Jalan Mesui) around the corner, and at which international and local musicians often jam.

Neighbour **Palate Palette** (21 Jalan Mesui, off Jalan Nagasari), which serves a selection of local and western food and drinks, is comfortably informal and always welcoming. Bangsar Baru's **Telawi Street Bistro** (1–3 Jalan Telawi Tiga, Bangsar Baru) cheekily serves up shots on spanking boards. Here, dancing is encouraged.

Just down the road, the smoke-free bar/art gallery **Attic** (61–2 Jalan Bangkung) hosts sing-along nights which are always fun. In nearby Damansara, **The Vintry** (130 Jalan Kasah, Medan Damansara) has a small but consistently good bar menu and a well-considered wine selection which makes it a necessity to always book in advance.

The hotels are also getting in on the action, with **Zeta Bar** (Hilton Kuala Lumpur, 3 Jalan Stesen Sentral) leading the pack with its much-vaunted international deejays and bands. Fast gaining momentum across town, the **SkyBar** (33rd floor, Traders Hotel, Kuala Lumpur), with its stunning view of the twin towers, is the bar to be at for stargazers, both literally and metaphorically. Not to be outdone, the **Qba** (The Westin Kuala Lumpur, 199 Jalan Bukit Bintang) is de rigueur for salsa fans and lovers of all things South American. Still in the golden triangle, the **Luna Bar** (34th floor, Menara Pan Global, off Jalan P Ramlee) also boasts a superb vista of the twin towers and a lovely pool, although swimming is strongly discouraged.

The relatively new **Marketplace** (4A Lorong Yap Kwan Seng) is another bar with a view, and small musical ensembles add character to the spacious yet intimate setting. For the

THIS PAGE (FROM TOP): Dancing the night away at a popular disco; salsa is all the rage in downtown Kuala Lumpur.
OPPOSITE: The dome-shaped architecture of Zouk Kuala Lumpur has incorporated a modern mix of Madrid and Mediterranean styles, and boasts a view of the famous Petronas Twin Towers.

young, or young at heart, **Velvet Underground** (Zouk, 113 Jalan Ampang) is where the action is. If you're really brave, dive in and join the teeming dancers at **Zouk** in the next room.

For the café society, **Chinoz on the Park** (G47 Suria KLCC, Kuala Lumpur City Centre) offers a selection of Mediterranean snacks, beers, and front row seats that overlook the musical fountain.

Foodies are encouraged to pay homage to the café in **House and Co** (Lot S15 2nd floor, Bangsar Shopping Centre, 285 Jalan Maarof) for local delights; the teatime curry puffs are extremely popular and are available from 3 pm. Lie-ins on weekends demand a leisurely breakfast locale, so head to **La Bodega Deli** (ground floor, 18 Jalan Telawi 2) where it seems most of KL have their first meal of the day.

west malaysia

There's plenty afoot these days in Penang, with the **Garage**—which houses several bars, cafes and clubs—leading the charge for a feisty after dark scene.

Beach Blanket Babylon (16 Lebuh Bishop) is quixotically charming, and homemade cakes, cocktails, local dishes and sandwiches can be consumed al fresco, or upstairs in 'bed'. The younger generation in Penang usually amp it up at **Glo** (A8 The Garage, 2 Penang Road), the city's hottest dance club, whilst those with a penchant for live music are more likely to head to **Slippery Senoritas** (Lot B3A, The Garage, 2 Penang Road).

For cocktails with a (sea) view, the lovingly restored **32 @ The Mansion** (32 Jalan Sultan Ahmad Shah), which has an outdoor terrace and a sea wall, is the best the island has to offer. Nyonya and fusion style cuisine are the order of the day at **Bagan Bar + Restaurant** (18 Jalan Bagan Jermal), also the venue for post-prandial jazz performances and Broadway hits by local musicians.

Down at the Weld Quay, the **QE2** (Penang Jetty) has plenty happening, whether for dinner, snacks, drinks or all-out partying. Sister outlets **Soho Freehouse** (50 Penang Road) and **Soho Beach Bar** (Batu Ferringhi Road) offer a good range of international beers, are more informal, and are the clubhouses of choice for local pool aficionados.

In Pulau Langkawi, the café/bar scene is eclectic, with an emphasis on island chic, the grand matriarch of which is **Nam Restaurant** (formerly known as Bon Ton at the Beach, Pantai Cenang, Langkawi). Its Chin Chin bar is replete with Asian charm and antiques, and a tapas and mezze menu and speciality coffee liqueurs can be taken indoors or outside on the sunset deck. Down the road, the **Casa del Mar** (Pantai Cenang, Langkawi) beachfront bar is one of the best spots on the island to nurse a margarita and watch the sunset.

Whilst not on the beach, the **Campor Campor** restaurant and bar (Pantai Cenang) is always welcoming and it has been voted one of Malaysia's best eateries. At the **Sunken Pool Bar** (Berjaya Langkawi Beach & Spa Resort, Burau Bay, Langkawi), simplicity is key. Tropical cocktails are house specials, and sunsets are the star attraction.

Although not strictly speaking cafés, places like **Sands** (Tanjung Rhu

Resort Langkawi, Mukim Ayer Hangat, Langkawi) and **The Pavilion** (The Datai Langkawi, Jalan Teluk Datai, Langkawi) qualify by virtue of their rustic outdoor setting, casual dining, and thoughtful wine lists. Down south in Ipoh, the **Indulgence Restaurant and Jazz Room** (15 Lorong Cecil Rae, Taman Canning, Ipoh), with a bistro, courtyard, Moroccan room and live jazz band on weekends, is an all-rounder with a loyal local following.

east malaysia

Marrying contemporary chic with traditional design elements, **Bing!** (84 Jalan Padungan, Chinatown, Kuching) offers patrons free wi-fi surfing and Illy coffee brewed by trained baristas. At **Senso** (Hilton Kuching Hotel, Jalan Tunku Abdul Rahman, Kuching), stylemeisters are spotted sipping speciality martinis and chilling out to French house and acid jazz cooked up by resident deejays. **Soho** (64 Jalan Padungan, Kuching) is defined by its earthy décor and eclectic musical selection whilst neighbouring **Grappa** (Jalan Padungan, Kuching) caters to a slighter younger crowd and the music ranges from house to '80s hits.

The **@mosphere Modern Dining** revolving restaurant and lounge (18th floor, Menara Tun Mustapha, Kota Kinabalu) serves Pacific Rim cuisine and cocktails, accompanied by a 360-degree view of Kota Kinabalu, the South China Sea and the Crocker Range. At the **Shenanigan's Fun Pub** (Hyatt Regency Kinabalu, Jalan Datuk Salleh Sulong, Kota Kinabalu), live bands are matched by the cool sea breezes that waft through this Irish-themed pub.

THIS PAGE (FROM TOP): Chime at Sheraton Langkawi Beach Resort takes on a different personality at night to become the hottest nightspot on the island; Velvet Undergrounds attracts a chic crowd and serves up some of the best cocktails in town.

OPPOSITE: SkyBar on the 33rd floor of Traders Hotel promises diners a cosmopolitan nightscene of the city.

best places

Deserted white sand beaches, dense rainforests and orang utan sanctuaries alongside colonial-era towns, a throbbing dance scene and some of the region's best food—these are some of the top few reasons to be in Malaysia.

kuala lumpur

Reducing KL to a handful of tourist spots overlooks the fact that the city's strength lies in aggregates—in living, breathing neighbourhoods saturated with the quirks and idiosyncrasies of its people. Walk the streets, watch the people, discover the shops, architecture and food. Bear in mind the ethnic character of each place, but also notice the subtleties as well as incongruities: from telephone services in the middle of Chinatown offering discount rates for calls to Kathmandu, to Arabic street signs in the middle of Bukit Bintang.

West of the Klang River is what has been termed KL's civic heart, where almost all of the city's grand colonial buildings are located. **Dataran Merdeka** on Jalan Raja is the city's old padang (playing field). Once the nucleus of the colonial district, it remains a popular venue for parades and public gatherings. **Lake Gardens**, to the west of the city centre, is the favoured spot for tai chi and lovers' strolls. Located within its grounds is **Carcosa Seri Negara**, the former residence of the highest-ranking British official in the Malay states and now one of the most exclusive hotels in the city.

Chinatown and Little India are the city's oldest commercial districts, encompassing the very site where the beginnings of Kuala Lumpur first emerged. **Jalan Petaling** has shaped Chinatown's reputation as a source for imitation goods, but the neighbourhood still retains some of its original street life and speciality stores. Amidst the shophouses on Jalan Tun HS Lee are the **Sri Mahamariamman Temple**, **Guandi Temple** and **Sze Yah Temple**, the city's first Chinese temple. The ornate **Chan clan association temple** can be found at the southern end of Jalan Petaling.

At the heart of **Little India** is Jalan Masjid India, one of the city's most colourful streets, with a string of Indian sari shops on one end and shops specialising in traditional Malay clothing on the other. **Jalan Tuanku Abdul Rahman** is known for textiles and carpets. The **Coliseum Café and Hotel** (98–100 Jalan Tuanku Abdul Rahman) is a KL institution known for its classic steaks and quaint waiting staff of old-timers.

The predominantly Tamil neighbourhood of **Brickfields** is distinguished for its excellent South Indian food and Indian speciality shops. Also found here is the grand **Sri Kandaswamy Temple** (3 Lorong Scott) and the **Temple of Fine Arts** (114 Jalan Berhala), a centre for Indian performing arts.

Bukit Bintang is the city's shopping district, with retail outlets ranging from luxury boutiques to small local businesses. **Changkat Bukit Bintang**, near the city's old red-light district, has a string of swanky bars, eateries and clubs located in remodelled townhouses—chief among them is **Frangipani Restaurant & Bar** (25 Changkat Bukit

THIS PAGE (FROM TOP): The spires of the Kuala Lumpur Railway Station frame some of KL's most distinctive landmarks—the Menara Maybank, KL Tower and Petronas Twin Towers; the Sze Yah Temple in Chinatown, Kuala Lumpur.
OPPOSITE: The lake in Titiwangsa Park in KL with the Petronas Twin Towers in the background..

Bintang). A few blocks away, **No Black Tie** (17 Jalan Mesui) regularly features local singer-songwriters and jazz musicians.

Surrounded by ghost stories and legends of local gangsters, the colonial-era **Pudu Jail** on Jalan Pudu has been the backdrop for some of the country's most dramatic and sensational events. Remnants of its famous mural—painted by inmates and said to be the longest in the world—can still be seen along the perimeter wall.

Located at the heart of the **KL City Centre** (KLCC), the **Petronas Twin Towers** are the city's claim to fame. At the foot of the towers is the **KLCC park**, an attractive public space that gets especially crowded on weekends. One of the hippest places to be seen at in town is **SkyBar** (33rd floor, Traders Hotel, Kuala Lumpur), which has a rooftop lap pool and sweeping vistas of the city. Nearby is **Zouk** (113 Jalan Ampang), one of the busiest dance clubs in the city. An enclave of Malay culture in KL, **Kampung Baru** is a traditional village located in the shadow of the Petronas Twin Towers.

For unfettered panaromas of the city, the highest point open to the public is the viewing deck of the **KL Tower** (2 Jalan Punchak, off Jalan P Ramlee), located some 276 m (905.5 ft) above ground level. The **Bukit Nanas Forest Reserve** at its base is the only patch of primary rainforest left in the city.

Further afield, Bangsar's **Telawi** neighbourhood is where the trendy and coiffed sit back for drinks and smoke cigarettes at dimly lit bars and lounges. Longstanding favourites include **La Bodega** (16 Jalan Telawi Dua), **Alexis** (29A Jalan Telawi Tiga) and **Telawi Street Bistro** (1–3 Jalan Telawi Tiga).

west malaysia

Batu Caves in Selangor bring together nature and religion in one place. A complex network of limestone caves, the site is best known for one cave in particular— the Temple Cave, where the colours and curves of Hindu sculptures are contrasted against the ragged contours of its rock formations. The cave is the site for the annual Thaipusam festival. Also in Selangor is the **Sepang International Circuit**, the venue for the annual Formula One Malaysian Grand Prix.

Pangkor Laut, a privately-owned island, is a luxury retreat off the coast of Perak. Its main draw is a string of resort villas built on stilts over the sea connected by wooden walkways. The island's entire 120 hectares (300 acres) is the exclusive preserve of the guests at the resort.

Located off the coast of Kedah, **Pulau Langkawi** offers far more than just spectacular beaches—other attractions include bird-watching opportunities (especially of rare eagles), scenic fishing villages and elegant resorts.

George Town, the hub of the former Straits Settlement of Penang, once attracted merchants from around the world, including Acehnese, Armenians, Siamese, Germans, Iraqis and Hadramis. More recently, it has carved out a reputation for itself as an enclave for heritage preservation, with historic streetscapes composed of shophouses, trade guild centres, colonial-era mansions, civic buildings as well as numerous places of

worship. Also found here are traditional trades and street performances such as Chinese opera and hand puppet shows.

Further south is the **Snake Temple** (Sungei Kluang), dedicated to a Buddhist monk and, more famously, a sanctuary for pit vipers. **Penang Hill**, which can be accessed by a funicular railway, provides panoramic views of the island and mainland West Malaysia.

Like Penang, **Melaka** is a hybrid of disparate cultures. The legacies of six centuries of conquerors and merchants—from the Portuguese to the Japanese—are evident in the city's architecture and syncretic communities.

Taman Negara in Pahang is one of the Peninsula's biggest draws, a lush 4,343 sq km (1,073,179 acres) of dense, pristine rainforest. **Gunung Tahan**, the highest peak in the Peninsula, is also located within the park. For a break from the tropical humidity, Pahang's **Cameron Highlands** offer cool weather and vast, undulating acres of plantations, including those of tea, flowers, vegetables and strawberries.

Pulau Tioman, off Pahang's coast, has the requisite white sand beaches as well as a forested interior. World War II battleships, reef sharks, turtles and a large variety of fish and coral make snorkelling and diving here particularly rewarding.

A little further north, a trinity of island retreats in Terengganu—**Pulau Perhentian, Pulau Lang Tengah** and **Pulau Redang**—offer more snorkelling and diving opportunities. Also in Terengganu is **Pulau Duyung**, the centre for traditional Malay boat building. It seems that the boats are built entirely from memory.

Kota Bharu is the cultural capital of the northeast and the last stronghold of regional crafts and performing arts, which include wayang kulit (shadow puppetry) and mak yong, the oldest surviving form of Malay dance theatre. Kota Bharu hosts several annual events, including bird-singing, kite-flying (a serious Kelantanese pastime), drumming and top-spinning contests.

The East-West Highway and the East Coast Railway line—both of which begin near Kota Bharu—offer two of the most scenic overland journeys that can be undertaken in the Peninsula.

east malaysia

Sarawak's rivers are lined with jungles, swamps, mangroves and longhouse communities that maintain much of their old way of life. The **Batang Rejang** and its tributaries are the stronghold of the Iban, although its upper reaches, along with those of the **Baram**, are primarily the domain of their old rivals, the Orang Ulu. Both are among the country's most spirited and hospitable people.

Sarawak is also the setting for the wildly popular Rainforest World Music Festival, an annual three-day long party at the **Sarawak Cultural Village** (Pantai Damai) that revolves around folk music, tuak (local rice wine) and other distractions, backdropped by the surrounding jungle and the imposing **Gunung Santubong**.

The **Semenggoh Wildlife Rehabilitation Centre** (Semenggoh

Nature Reserve) is one of the best places to see a shaggy 100-kg (220-lb) Borneo orang utan up close, without the obstruction of safety barriers. In the northeast, the **Gunung Mulu National Park** is a sprawling reserve with several natural features, including the Sarawak Chamber, the world's largest single cave chamber, and the jagged limestone peaks of the Pinnacles. The reserve has several trails for hikers, including the Headhunters' Trail, named after the route used in the past by tribal war parties.

At 4,095 m (13,435 ft), **Mount Kinabalu** in Sabah is Southeast Asia's highest peak. Over 1,000 species of orchids as well as pitcher plants, rhododendrons, rafflesias, laurels and magnolias can be found here.

The three islands that make up the **Turtle Islands National Park** off the coast of Sandakan are the nesting grounds of two species of endangered sea turtles. The park provides visitors with the rare chance of watching the turtles nest under the cover of darkness.

Pulau Sipadan is widely regarded as the region's most exciting diving destination, teeming with turtles and schools of barracuda, tuna, manta rays and hammerhead sharks. Among the island's most popular dive sites is the **Hanging Gardens**, an underwater cliff carpeted with soft coral.

Finally, Sabah's **Kinabatangan Wildlife Sanctuary** offers some of the best chances to spot wildlife, including all eight species of Bornean hornbills, crocodiles, deer, proboscis monkeys, wild cats, orang utans and pygmy elephants.

THIS PAGE (FROM TOP): Sabah's Kinabatangan Wildlife Sanctuary was gazetted in 2005 to protect wildlife, such as Borneo's unique subspecies of the Asian elephant; tropical fish swim amongst coral in the waters off Pulau Sipadan.

OPPOSITE (FROM TOP, LEFT): An elderly Iban man seated on the verandah of a traditional longhouse in Sarawak; Kelantanese wayang kulit (Wayang Kulit Siam) is the principal form of shadow puppetry in Malaysia; a craftsman in Kota Bharu, Kelantan, making a traditional kite known locally as wau.

dining

Malaysia has an astonishing array of food under one proverbial roof. In addition to the well-known ethnic mix of Malay, Chinese and Indian communities, there is the culinary input of its recent immigrants. Although derivatives of Malaysian cuisine exist all over the world, there is no better place than the homeland for trying out the real thing. Local cuisine is as varied as the country's ethnic components, which go far beyond the generic Malay, Chinese and Indian fare. Often it is a combination of all these diverse elements.

The Malays of the northern states incorporate Thai influences in their cooking, while those in the south favour thick and creamy dishes with an occasional Arabic twist. Chinese food encompasses everything from the subtle nuances of Cantonese fare to the fire of Szechuan dishes and the earthy, farmhouse tastes imported by Hakka people. The distinctive blend of Malay and Chinese that comes together as 'Baba-Nyonya' culture is equally noticeable in their food. Indian cuisine in Malaysia is marked by the raw spices of the south, moderated with liberal quantities of rice and coconut milk, or powdered spices of the north in yoghurt-based dishes accompanied by bread.

There are also the almost-forgotten cuisines of the smaller ethnic minorities. When the Portuguese conquered the Malay Peninsula in 1511, they left a legacy of distinctive food. The flagship dish is the slightly sour and very spicy 'devil curry', which is hard to find outside the Portuguese enclave in Melaka.

Similarly, the simple tastes of Borneo's tribes are something of a rarity outside the few longhouses that remain.

The common factor among every type of local cuisine is that the best places to enjoy them are the home or the humblest commercial outlets. The comparatively egalitarian nature of Malaysian society means there is no shame—or health risk—attached to eating at hawker stalls. There are some dishes that cannot be prepared properly in the kitchen of the smartest restaurants. Satay is one example, due to the health-and-safety regulations imposed on hotels. These sticks of meat with peanut sauce can only be truly savoured when cooked on the street over an open charcoal fire. Gastronomes in search of stylish surroundings and cutting-edge cuisine will also find that Malaysia is their multi-national oyster; there are many restaurants of the highest quality here.

kuala lumpur + petaling jaya

Western food dominates the top end of Malaysian dining. For more than 20 years, **Lafite** (Lobby, Shangri-La Hotel, Kuala Lumpur, 11 Jalan Sultan Ismail) has been a byword for the finest dining in KL. The restaurant serves exquisite French food with the occasional twist. As with all the Asian hotels owned by Malaysian billionaire Robert Kuok, Lafite has a wine list that is as premier cru as its name suggests. French food is also available at **The Dining Room** (Carcosa Seri Negara, Taman Tasik Perdana, Persiaran Mahameru), although its true raison d'etre is the setting rather

than the food. The presence of a French chef has improved the offerings, but what most visitors will revel in is the history that infuses this house, which was built by Sir Frank Swettenham, the first Resident-General of the Federated Malay States. Fine dining can have a fun side too. **Prego** (The Westin Kuala Lumpur, 199 Jalan Bukit Bintang) presents Italian food with a light touch and plenty of good humour. The open kitchen sets the informal mood; fortunately though, the staff are no longer gleefully handing out comical red noses! The cheerful mood is maintained at **El Cerdo** (43–45 Changkat Bukit Bintang), which specialises in breaking plates after they have been used to serve up a suckling pig. This restaurant is part of a vigorous rearguard action by pork lovers. Chef-owner Werner Kuhn has made a real statement with a restaurant whose name means 'the pig' in Spanish.

Western and local dishes are served side by side at **Alexis** (1st floor, Bangsar Shopping Centre), a small, simple bistro that attracts a very smart crowd. This is where captains of industry and the arts gather for good food in unpretentious surroundings. Malaysia's most celebrated chef, Ken Hoh, started his own establishment on the third floor (hence its name, **Third Floor**) of the Marriott Hotel. Chef Hoh produces sublime combinations that team up the lightest and freshest Asian ingredients with the heavier Continental flavours of foie gras and truffle. There is a trace of fusion at **Sao Nam** (25 Jalan Tingkat Tong Shin),

THIS PAGE (FROM TOP, LEFT): Alexis has made a name for itself over the years by providing good food in informal surroundings; Vietnamese food has become popular over the past few years, with Sao Nam leading the way; Third Floor restaurant at the JW Marriott Hotel is supervised by Malaysia's celebrated chef, Ken Hoh. OPPOSITE: The Dining Room offers the most historic surroundings of any restaurant in KL.

which incorporates old-time French favourites such as canard à l'orange. Otherwise the food is all about the fresh, simple tastes of Vietnam. This restaurant is by far the best exponent of Vietnamese cuisine, with an ambience to match. Chef Tien does wonderful work with Vietnamese classics, bringing in local ingredients to create unforgettable but highly seasonal dishes such as mangosteen salad. Offerings from the less-explored corners of Indo-China are available at **Tamarind Springs** (Jalan 1 Taman TAR). The setting is a tropical fairytale, especially in the evening, with verandahs hanging over a vast expanse of greenery (which is actually a golf course).

Golf is not the lure for diners at **Iketeru** (Hilton Kuala Lumpur, 3 Jalan Stesen Sentral). Rather, this Japanese restaurant is prospering with Chef Ricky and his subtle updating of traditional classics. The setting is even more avant-garde than the food. **Wasabi Bistro** at the super-smart Mandarin Oriental also does remarkable things with Japanese food, combining it with Hawaiian offerings in a medley that works well in tropical Malaysia. Travelling celebrities such as Ronan Keating enjoy it for its privacy.

For a tasting sampler of Asia, there is **EEST** at the Westin Hotel. Japanese, Thai, Chinese, Vietnamese and Malaysian dishes are available in surroundings that are laid-back but luxurious. Staying close to the flavours of home, Starhill Shopping Centre takes the Malaysian 'food court' concept to an entirely new level. There are numerous outlets in this food village, which is located in the basement, with **Fisherman's Cove** being particularly worthy of mention. Seafood is a local favourite, executed with creativity here. The neighbourhood's most influential landlord, Tan Sri Francis Yeoh, is a frequent visitor.

For traditional Malaysian food in the style of old Penang—with a building to match—**Old China Café** (11 Jalan Balai Polis, Kuala Lumpur) offers a trip back in time. It is located near the historic Petaling Street. Diners in pursuit of Malay cuisine must head for **Bijan** (3 Jalan Ceylon). This is one of the very few outlets that put fine dining into Malay food. There is also the unusual opportunity of enjoying it with wine. The menu takes few liberties with the all-time greats of Malay gastronomy although things get more innovative with desserts that include a chocolate durian cheesecake.

west malaysia

Penang has a longer history of culinary connoisseurship than anywhere else in Malaysia, and **Feringgi Grill** (Batu Ferringhi Beach) has been the island's top restaurant since 1973. This is the oldest fine dining venue in the country. Grill rooms are now almost extinct in Malaysia, which makes Feringgi Grill a bit of living history with its baronial atmosphere. It also features that other endangered species: the band of strolling musicians. At the even older Eastern & Oriental Hotel is **The 1885**, the only contender to the Feringgi Grill's haute cuisine crown in the northern states of Malaysia. Here, the gourmet tradition is still alive with superb soups, such as the perennal favourite, mushroom soup, and the requisite wagyu beef. At **The Smokehouse** (Tanah Rata), in the chilly surroundings of Cameron Highlands, there is also the feel of old England. The building dates back to 1939 and the restaurant serves food from the era, including chicken in the basket. It also serves the rare cream tea of yesteryear with scones, but minus clotted cream. Local society folk and tourists find it irresistible. Neighbouring Genting Highlands, the entertainment capital of Malaysia, is an hour's drive from KL and has several restaurants for high rollers. The best of them is **The Olive** (Genting Hotel), which makes a serious effort to be innovative and exemplary. Its quest to present the best of contemporary cuisine is backed up by a procession of guest chefs from overseas, including Volker Drkosch and Joel Antunes.

Asian food also finds a superior forum at a few restaurants in West Malaysia. Langkawi is a playground for those in pursuit of a gentler pace of life, and nowhere is the easy-going spirit of this island better embodied than by **Nam Restaurant** (Pantai Cenang). Formerly known as Bon Ton at the Beach, it has glorious fusion food that incorporates everything from Nyonya specialities to the definitive chocolate dessert. A little further along the Langkawi coast is **The Gulai House**, part of The Andaman resort. This location is extremely upmarket and much frequented by the Formula One Grand Prix frontrunners. The Gulai House

THIS PAGE (FROM TOP, LEFT): Nam Restaurant makes the most of Langkawi's island-paradise status, offering food to match; few restaurants in Malaysia combine classic local dishes with colonial-era atmosphere with as much success as Old China Café; the Gulai House at The Andaman provides Malay and Indian cuisines in a unique beach-side setting.

OPPOSITE: Asian food is presented in the most stylish surroundings at Eest; a view of the great outdoors is one of the main attractions of Tamarind Springs.

serves Malay and Indian food, with the lapping of the Andaman Sea just beyond the walls of this nipah-roofed restaurant. The food has been tamed for the benefit of the mainly foreign clientele.

east malaysia

East Malaysia is all about informality, although Kuching, the capital of Sarawak, does offer opportunities for fine dining, compared with Kota Kinabalu, capital of the neighbouring state of Sabah. For Italian food in Kuching, nothing beats the fare at **Beccari** (Merdeka Palace Hotel), which was until recently supervised by Chef Vittorio, who used to run the popular Trebotti restaurant in KL years ago. The other place for Kuching haute cuisine is the **Steakhouse** (Hilton Kuching). This is the place where Sarawak's powerbrokers chow down on more than just steak, as there are many other meat dishes available, including Mongolian lamb. The inventive sorbet features indigenous Sarawak black pepper. For more samples of authentic Sarawak flavours, there is **Chia Heng** (5A Lorong Datuk Abang Abdul Rahim) restaurant. It specialises in Teochew cuisine and uses mainly seafood for its ingredients. Some argue that, like many other Chinese restaurants in Malaysia, Chia Heng's results are possibly better than those that some five-star hotels can deliver!

In Sabah, the place where Kota Kinabalu's hip crowd congregates to dine and be seen is **@tmosphere Modern Dining** (18th floor, Menara Tun Mustapha, Jalan Sulaman). Amazing views and an equally eye-catching retro interior design compete for attention. Pacific Rim is the theme, although Malaysian favourites are also available. Located in the same city, **Ferdinand's** (Sutera Harbour Resort) serves perhaps the best food in East Malaysia, and definitely provides the best service. The Singaporean owner of the Sutera Harbour Resort, Datuk Edward Ong, has turned it into a tourist magnet and of its many outlets, the creative Italian fare at Ferdinand's truly stands out. Another outstanding restaurant close to Kota Kinabalu is **Coast** (Shangri-La's Rasa Ria Resort), which serves the contemporary Western cuisine that is so popular throughout Malaysia. The emphasis at Coast used to be Californian but the menu has evolved to become more broadly Western. Rather unusually, the chef is from England.

Malaysia's colonial past is most keenly felt in Borneo. **The English Tea House** (2002 Jalan Istana, Sandakan) is the place for a varied selection of quintessential English delicacies, from cream tea with scones to a full meal incorporating fish and chips. The establishment is upscale but offers excellent value, in addition to a nostalgic experience. **Port View** (Jalan Tun Fuad Stephens Road, Kota Kinabalu) may not feature the same colonial charm as The English Tea House, but this does not detract from the appeal of its seafood menu. The preparation of dishes is superb and only the freshest ingredients are used. Ultimately, seafood is a special sort of gastronomic passion and the people of Sabah are more interested in the food than the façade.

THIS PAGE (FROM TOP): Retro chic rules at Kota Kinabalu's liveliest fine-dining outlet, @tmosphere Modern Dining; one of Borneo's best Western restaurants, Ferdinand's also offers a romantic location next to the ocean.

OPPOSITE: The Four Seasons Resort in Langkawi exudes global glamour with a liberal dose of local charm at outlets such as the Rhu Bar.

fashion + designers

For dedicated followers of fashion and aspiring designers with a vision, there's no better place to be right now than Malaysia. More than ever, high luxe malls housing chic boutiques proliferate the burgeoning retail paradise that is Kuala Lumpur, and international couture names are inspiration for fashion-forward local designers to realise their dream of dressing Malaysians in all things beautiful.

Four-year-old **Malaysian International Fashion Alliance**'s (C139 KL Plaza Court, Jalan Bukit Bintang, Kuala Lumpur) crusade is to introduce Malaysian fashion designers to the world and to establish Malaysia as a key international fashion destination. Its annual Malaysia International Fashion Week (M-IFW) has showcased many emerging talents and placed them firmly on the fashion radar. The 2007 show, titled KL Six, featured the latest collections of leading Malaysian designers Sonny San, Melinda Looi, Datuk Tom Abang Saufi, Eric Choong, Rizalman Ibrahim and Radzuan Radziwill to an enthusiastic audience. In homes around Malaysia, viewers tune in weekly to the travails of ambitious young designers who are mentored by stalwarts of the fashion industry.

Kuala Lumpur's other fashion week is the Kuala Lumpur Fashion Week (KLFW), which is organised by the non-profit Malaysian Official Designers' Association (MODA). Formed to nurture the growth of the Malaysian fashion industry, and to provide a viable platform for young fashion designers, MODA's KLFW 2006 highlighted the collections of such designers as Key Ng, Khoon Hooi, Melinda Looi and Zang Toi.

couture

Dubbed Malaysia's Prince of Fashion, Paris-trained **Datuk Bernard Chandran** is a regular at London Fashion Week and owns a store in Knightsbridge that showcases his couture designs. His enduring appeal is largely due to his ability to innovate and reinvent, so that traditional textures and styles such as the Malay baju kurung and sarung kebaya are transformed into chic, contemporary clothes with distinctive silhouettes (Bernard Chandran Flagship Boutique, 2nd floor, KL Plaza, 179 Jalan Bukit Bintang).

The glamorous and feminine designs of New York-based **Zang Toi** have made him the darling of the Hollywood set. His Malaysian boutiques marry fashion with the café life and variously carry his ready-to-wear designs, couture or working attire (Zang Toi boutique, Bangsar Shopping Centre and Great Eastern Mall).

The unconventional style of **Melinda Looi** first thrust her into the public psyche when she was awarded the MIFA Designer of the Year award in 2004, and again in 2006. Now endeared by royals and stars alike, Looi's couture line has expanded to include the Mel diffusion line and a bridal range (Melinda Looi Couture, 279 Jalan Maarof, Bangsar).

Malaysia's most famous export, Dato **Jimmy Choo** and his iconic shoes need little introduction. Although he is no longer involved in the ready-to-wear range (Jimmy Choo, KLCC), Choo continues to hand-make shoes for the glitterati from his workshop in

London's Connaught Street and is presently helping to establish a shoemaking institute in Malaysia.

KL-based **Eric Choong**'s couture creations are deeply influenced by Malaysian culture, but always updated with contemporary detailing. Choong's penchant for batik has also established him as one of the leading exponents of reviving and modernising this traditional fabric. Apart from his couture creations, Choong also designs bridal wear (61–1 Jalan Telawi Tiga).

Also noted for the Asian—specifically Sarawakian (her home state)—cultural references that flow through her designs, **Datuk Tom Abang Saufi**'s creations are floaty and bold. They eschew zips and buttons for 'maximum style and minimum fuss'. Her fans run the gamut of professions, from politician's wife (Cherie Blair) to singers and actresses.

Perak-born **Khoon Hooi**, recently bestowed the International Recognition Award at the 2007 Bangkok International Fashion Week, is known for his prodigious use of natural fabrics which integrate seamlessly with his flirtatious yet paradoxically innocent designs. Apart from his diffusion Inspire line, and bridal couture, Khoon Hooi's range will soon include men's wear (Explore Floor, Starhill Gallery, The Gardens Mid Valley; Inspire, 1st floor, Sungei Wang Plaza).

Beatrice Looi is a veteran of the rag trade with more than 18 years in the industry. Her signature flowing gowns are by and large handcrafted with plenty of bead and crystal work. Her Spring/Summer 2008 collection was a tribute to the jazz era and the roaring twenties, and hailed a return to the designer's predilection for all things vintage (Starhill, Jalan Bukit Bintang, and 1st floor, Bangsar Village II).

ready to wear

Retailing around the world, the ready-to-wear Eclipse range by **Sonny San** is defined by its chameleon-like ability to constantly evolve and its perennially assured but feminine designs. The range includes a variety of accessories, shoes, bags, and a Couture Eclipse Luxe line, and there is something for virtually every taste (KLCC, Lot 10, Mid Valley Megamall, 1 Utama, Sunway Pyramid, The Gardens Mid Valley, and Pavilion in Kuala Lumpur, and Maylana in Kota Kinabalu).

Established in 2003, **Farah Khan** is the brainchild of Dato Farah Khan, president of the Melium Group. It has for the last 18 years—through the introduction of such international brands as Pucci, Lacroix, Zegna and Boss—been the arbiter of good sartorial taste in Malaysia. Available around the world, Farah Khan's philosophy lies in its reinterpretation of timeless classics to produce 'effortlessly chic' dresses, with organic and geometric motifs in intricate beadwork (Aseana, Suria KLCC).

The trick to relative newcomer **Key Ng**'s designs lies in the detailing of his futuristic, often funky clothing for men and women. Locally sourced and manufactured, his clothing range includes couture, work attire, sportswear, and bridal wear (Key Ng, 1 Utama, The Curve; men's wear, 1st floor, Sungei Wang Plaza, Avenue K, Isetan KLCC, Isetan Lot 10; ladies, lower ground floor, Sungei Wang Plaza).

THIS PAGE (FROM TOP): Jimmy Choo is known for its glamorous accessories, favoured by international stars; jewel-studded accessories are must-haves to give a complete elegant look; popular designer wear by Eric Choong, one of the 'KL Six'.

OPPOSITE: A model showcases an outfit by designer Melinda Looi at the 'KL Six' galas during the Malaysian-International Fashion Week.

galleries, museums + theatres

Malaysia has been working hard to put itself on the world cultural map in recent years. More museums are being built and the public has become more 'art-aware'. The emphasis is on contemporary art and cultural activities that mainly take place in air-conditioned comfort.

kuala lumpur

A starting point for Malaysian heritage is the **National Museum** (Jalan Damansara), which has recently undergone a makeover. Founded 50 years ago, it has become a national icon filled with Malaysia's natural and cultural history, where wildlife exhibits and dioramas of the significant moments in the country's history are showcased. Round the corner is one of Malaysia's newest and most exciting cultural stops—**Islamic Arts Museum Malaysia** (Jalan Lembah Perdana)— filled with light, space and Asia's best collection of Islamic art. It is a magnet for international dignitaries eager to understand the highly topical issue of Islamic culture. Moving from the colonial charm of the Lake Gardens to the high-tech bustle of Kuala Lumpur City Centre, there is the **Galeri PETRONAS** (341–343 Ampang Mall, Suria KLCC). Located in a prestigious shopping mall, this gallery is run by Malaysia's national petroleum company. It regularly puts up contemporary thought-provoking art exhibitions, and is the ideal spot for some quiet contemplation in the midst of the shopping frenzy. Next door is KL's most serious commercial gallery for regional antiques. **Pucuk Rebung** (302A Ampang Mall, Suria KLCC) sells everything from Malay textiles to Bornean idols and combines this with a private museum of mainly Kelantanese royal memorabilia. Slightly further out from the 'Golden Triangle' of downtown KL is the **National Art Gallery** (2 Jalan Temerloh, off Jalan Tun Razak). For many years this was housed in a converted hotel but has had its own dedicated building since 2000. The collection provides an unrivalled overview of Malaysian art.

Art lovers looking for glamorous exhibition openings can head for **Valentine Willie Fine Art** (1st floor, 17 Jalan Telawi Tiga). This is the most

innovative gallery in Malaysia and promotes the country's leading young artists. A recent rival is the **Wei-Ling Gallery** (8 Jalan Scott) in up-and-coming Brickfields, owned by the daughter of Malaysia's leading environmental architect. Equally advanced, but without the generous wine and canape launches, is **Annexe@Central Market**. This is a venue, rather than a gallery, but it consistently puts on the most surprising and avant-garde shows.

In recent years, efforts to raise cultural standards have been made. The **Malaysian Philharmonic Orchestra** (MPO), housed in the Petronas Twin Towers, is one good example. Since its inaugural performance in 1998, the MPO has evolved into one of Asia's best orchestras and a well-known player in the international arena of classical music. The opening of the **Kuala Lumpur Performing Arts Centre** (KL Pac), or Pantai Seni KL, in 2005 marked a new beginning for the performing arts in Malaysia. Its programme comprising dramas, dances and music is varied, offering local as well as international productions. **The Actors Studio** (T116 Bangsar Shopping Centre, 3rd floor, 285 Jalan Maarof, Bukit Bandaraya) has over the decade staged numerous quality plays such as *Hamlet* (2005) and *Dangerous Liaisons* (2001).

west malaysia

Just outside the nation's capital are some quirky cultural hotspots. The **Royal Selangor Pewter Museum** (Setapak Jaya) is where one can learn about Malaysia's most special metal. In addition to a wide range of antique pewter, there are also interactive activities. At the other end of the Klang Valley is the **Shah Alam Gallery** (Shah Alam Lake Gardens), a lakeside location with a comprehensive selection of contemporary Malaysian art. The most established art tradition is found in the northern Malaysian state of Penang. The **Penang Museum** (Lebuh Farquhar) specialises in the island's relatively long and interesting history. Near Penang is the holiday island of Langkawi, home to the eponymous **Ibrahim Hussein Museum and Cultural Foundation**. Established by the country's leading artist, this is a gallery dedicated to his work. A good test for any society is its ability to laugh at itself, and the **Instant Café Theatre** (1 Jalan 10/12, off Jalan Gasing, Petaling Jaya, Selangor) is a testament to this, although its political satire has undoubtedly ruffled some feathers!

east malaysia

East Malaysia has quite a different heritage from Peninsular Malaysia. The tribal traditions of Borneo are well represented at the **Sarawak Museum** (Kuching), which is one of the oldest museums in Malaysia. On a less serious note, the **Cat Museum** was established in Kuching in 1993. (Incidentally, the Malay word for cat is 'kucing'.) **Nelson's Gallery**, on Jalan Main Bazaar, owned by the flamboyant Nelson Tan, is packed to the ceiling with surprising artefacts—beads, textiles, jewellery and ceramics. The **Sabah Museum** in Kota Kinabalu, the only museum in Sabah, houses historical state artefacts.

THIS PAGE (FROM TOP): The Wei-Ling Gallery is among the newest and most exciting of Kuala Lumpur's commercial galleries; traditional Malay music is seldom heard these days except at official functions and in tourist settings.

OPPOSITE (FROM TOP): The KL Performing Arts Centre is part of the new generation of avant-garde art venues. It occupies an uniquely 'green' location in the centre of a park; the tiles that decorate the Islamic Arts Museum Malaysia were specially made in Iran and installed by Iranian artisans.

shopping

Malaysia has some of the region's glossiest shopping malls and some of its most colourful markets. Kuala Lumpur has everything from Italian handbags and Kenyan coffee beans to local spices and traditional aphrodisiacs. Throughout West and East Malaysia, regional differences give each market its own character

and its own unique specialties, from batik and songket in Kuala Terengganu to machetes and Bajau ponies in Kota Belud.

kuala lumpur

With a concentration of nine shopping centres in an area little more than 1 sq km (0.39 sq miles),

the **Bukit Bintang** neighbourhood is the city's most important shopping belt. The high-end of the Jalan Bukit Bintang shopping spectrum can be found at the intersection with Jalan Raja Chulan. Opened in 2007, the **Pavilion Kuala Lumpur** (168 Jalan Bukit Bintang) is the gleaming addition to the neighbourhood, with

stores that include Kiehl's, Juicy Couture, Bebe, Versace and Chloe. Across the street is **Starhill Gallery** (181 Jalan Bukit Bintang), which hosts the sole Malaysian outlets of luxury brands such as Jaeger-LeCoultre, Van Cleef & Arpels, Kenzo and Anne Klein. With a cube-shaped storefront studded with LEDs, Louis Vuitton's

flagship store extends onto the sidewalk like a diamond-encrusted treasure chest.

Some 100 m (328 ft) away is the undulating green façade of **Lot 10** (50 Jalan Sultan Ismail) and, beyond it, **Sungei Wang Plaza** (99 Jalan Bukit Bintang). The oldest mall on the strip, and one of the busiest, Sungei Wang is something of an enclave for all things plastic, cheap and colourful, from cartoon-imprinted handphone accessories to quirky handbags. Right next door, **BB Plaza** (111 Jalan Bukit Bintang) has kiosks and stalls selling everything from Arab perfume to feng shui crystals. Also located in the neighbourhood are **KL Plaza** (179 Jalan Bukit Bintang), **Low Yat Plaza** (7 Jalan Bintang, off Jalan Bukit Bintang) and **Berjaya Times Square** (1 Jalan Imbi).

KL's commercial district extends further north to **Suria KLCC** (Kuala Lumpur City Centre), wedged between the colossal **Petronas Twin Towers**. KLCC has all the familiar names in fashion, electronics and home decor, as well as **Aseana**, which houses an exquisite selection of Southeast Asian-made and -inspired fashion, from deconstructed kebaya to airy chiffon dresses with batik prints. On the third floor, **Pucuk Rebung Gallery Museum** has a collection of handcrafted goods that is as much a lesson in Malaysian history and ethnography as it is a shopping experience.

Further afield, Bangsar's **Jalan Telawi** may be better known for its nightlife, but the area is also thriving with colourful boutiques flaunting styles that range from French

boudoir to Sex-Pistols punk. At the end of the street, **Silverfish Books** (58–1 Jalan Telawi Tiga) is a popular local-owned bookstore with solid literati credentials. Nearby, **Bangsar Shopping Centre** (285 Jalan Maarof), is a hub for expatriates and affluent locals. Adding to the array of shopping opportunities in the neighbourhood are **Bangsar Village** (1 Jalan Telawi Satu), and its more upscale affiliate, **Bangsar Village II** (2 Jalan Telawi Satu).

Other major shopping malls in KL are **Mid Valley Megamall** (Mid Valley City, Lingkaran Syed Putra) and **1 Utama Shopping Centre** (1 Lebuh Bandar Utama, Bandar Utama).

THIS PAGE (FROM TOP): Located at the foot of the Petronas Twin Towers, Suria KLCC is one of the city's most popular shopping destinations; the variety of books available in Malaysia reflects the diversity of languages used by the country's polyglot population.

OPPOSITE: The ubiquity of Western brands and images around Kuala Lumpur reflects the preferences and expanding wallets of Malaysian consumers.

shopping

Jalan Petaling, situated in the heart of Chinatown, has a reputation for knockoffs. Look beyond the imitation goods, however, and Chinatown does indeed live up to its name, with shops and stalls that still sell traditional Chinese medicine, local coffee, freshly-baked Chinese pastries and old-fashioned ceramic ware.

Something of a well-kept city secret are the Nepalese gemstone traders on Jalan Petaling. Occupying several shoplots, the merchants sit behind individual desks blanketed with wares ranging from Indian-made bracelets to uncut Afghan lapis lazuli. Just a few streets away is **Central Market** (Jalan Hang Kasturi), offering all variety of souvenirs and trinkets geared towards tourists.

North of Chinatown is **Jalan Masjid India**, which has rows of shops selling saris, jasmine-scented soap, coconut oil, Indian astrology guides and DVDs of the latest Tamil and Hindi blockbusters. At the southern end of Jalan Masjid India is **Wisma Yakin**, one of the best places to get tailor-made Malay attire. Out on the street, vendors sell everything from the Quran to tongkat ali, a traditional Malay aphrodisiac. Just one street away, on **Jalan Tuanku Abdul Rahman**, are businesses that specialise in textiles, offering yards of satin, chiffon, lace and cotton printed with designs ranging from the glorious to the garish. **Asoka Palaikat** (7 Jalan Tuanku Abdul Rahman) is a store specialising in traditional plaid sarong.

KL's produce markets are wet, steamy, crowded affairs. Among the busiest markets in the city are those in **Chow Kit** and **Pudu**.

On any given night, there is a pasar malam (night market) somewhere in the city. In addition to street food, items for sale include cooking utensils, rat traps, lingerie and Spongebob Squarepants pillows.

west malaysia
Throughout the rest of Peninsular Malaysia, shops and markets reflect the character and idiosyncrasies of the local population.

In Penang, the eclectic identity of the old Straits Settlement free port is evident throughout its capital of George Town. **S.M. Badjenid & Sons** (184 Lebuh Pantai), which was founded in 1917 by a merchant from Hadhramaut, specialises in essential oils and perfume blends. Jalan Penang, Lebuh Chulia and Jalan Masjid Kapitan Kling have shops cluttered with Straits-era antiques and curios.

The **Little Penang Street Market** on Upper Penang Road (Jalan Penang) is a community initiative promoting the local arts, crafts and culture. Held on the last Sunday of every month, the market features both traditional and contemporary crafts, such as Chinese dough figurines and custom-made handbags.

A much older, but no less colourful, market is the daily **Chowrasta Market** on Jalan Penang, known in particular for having a good variety of preserved nutmegs and other Penang food specialties. The **Lorong Kulit flea market**, which has not quite shaken off its reputation as a thieves' market, has old vinyl records, brassware and collectible coins.

Another former Straits Settlement is Melaka. The town has one of the only shops in the world that still produces shoes for bound feet: **Wah Aik** (56 Jalan Tokong) is fronted with a sign that reads 'Bound Feet Shoes (Original Pattern)'.

On the east coast, **Pasar Payang** (Jalan Sultan Abidin, Kuala Terengganu) is a busy local market located along the Terengganu River. The market is popular for its fresh produce as well as its selection of locally-made batik and songket. Kelantan's **Pasar Besar Siti Khadijah** (Kota Bharu) is perhaps West Malaysia's most photogenic market. In a large central atrium, women vendors sit on raised platforms surrounded by a mosaic of vegetables and fruits. The market also has a section devoted to textiles and another to kris and the other traditional weapons.

east malaysia

While Kuching's **Main Bazaar** is lined with shop after shop cluttered with Iban warrior sculptures in three different sizes, it is difficult to find genuine artefacts and well-crafted goods. One exception in Kuching is the **ARTrageously Ramsay Ong Gallery** (94 Main Bazaar), which has a fine, if limited, selection of new and old crafts.

In Sarawak, the meat section of a market can resemble an exhibition of local zoology. Alongside more conventional fare are pythons, wild boar, sting ray and live snails squirming in plastic bags (keep in mind, however, that the trade in wild game is a major ecological

concern). A good place to start is at the **Sunday market on Jalan Satok**, Kuching.

Markets beyond Kuching tend to strongly reflect the unique character of the local community. In the Melanau stronghold of Mukah, for instance, the community's long association with sago cultivation is evident everywhere in the local market, which has everything from sago flour and sago worms to baskets made of sago fibres.

In Sabah, the **tamu** is traditionally where various ethnic groups come together to trade and exchange news, and the **Sunday tamu on the outskirts of Kota Belud** is legendary. In addition to produce and household items, traders also sell home-grown tobacco, machetes and Bajau ponies. At the end of every year, a grand tamu, the **Tamu Besar Kota Belud**, takes place over two or three days.

Also of note are the tamu in Dongonggon, Tuaran, Tamparuli and Ranau, while **Kota Kinabalu's Sunday morning market on Jalan Gaya** is an urban version of the tamu.

THIS PAGE: A popular produce market, Pasar Besar Siti Khadijah is also one of Kota Bharu's main tourist attractions.

OPPOSITE (FROM LEFT, TOP): Textiles, jewellery, beads and pottery were among some of the earliest trade goods in Peninsular Malaysia. Today, each of those things can still be found in the shopping districts and marketplaces of Malaysia, albeit in more contemporary manifestations.

nature

Malaysia has a verdant landscape that is brimming with primordial regalia. Its rainforests are considered the oldest in the world, and they are home to over 15,000 flowering plant and 185,000 animal species. Its islands are simply picturesque, glistening in their azure, emerald and topaz hues—such a concentrated biodiversity has long been recognised as a priceless gift from Providence. Myths and legends abound, and they meander all the way to rarefied Himalayan heights.

According to some accounts, a mythical kingdom called Shambhala once existed amidst those snow-tipped peaks, and it reportedly had a garden called Malaya right in the centre of it, endowed with luscious plants and fruits that could only be found in the tropics. Legends are often the filtered truth of ages past; much like mottled sunrays in dense forest foliage. And the Malaysian rainforest is unlike any other: be it in the Peninsula, in Borneo, or right in the heart of the capital city, Kuala Lumpur.

kuala lumpur

Though Malaysia's landscape is dotted with unique limestone hills, there is one particular craggy outcrop made of quartz located on the outskirts of Kuala Lumpur, skirting the national zoo in Taman Melawati. The **Klang Gates Ridge**, or the **Tabur Ridge**, is a geologic anomaly. It is the longest quartz ridge in the world, measuring 16 km (10 miles) long and averaging 200 m (0.12 miles) wide. Due to its singularity, there are calls to list the ridge as a World Heritage Site. The quartz found here is reportedly of crystal-glass quality.

There are at least 265 distinct plant species along this ridge, with five of them endemic to the region. Some unique species here include the Malaysian peacock, fan palm and the endangered serow. Despite appearing to have an imposing jagged surface, Tabur Ridge is actually a hiker's haven, offering both easy and challenging routes. One can park his car at the foot of the hill, and literally trek one's way to **Janda Baik** in the state of Pahang. Black panthers have also been spotted in this area—an added thrill.

If a more relaxing experience is needed—and one free of unexpected arboreal menace—just relax at the base of the foothill and bask besides the shimmering waters of the **Klang Gates Dam**. One can hire a boat here from a nearby village, and take in a spot of fishing right in the middle of the lake. Caution is advised though. What lies beneath includes the large Toman (snakehead) fish.

Consisting of some 600 hectares (1,482.6 acres) of tropical forest, the **Forest Research Institute Malaysia** in Kepong, Selangor can be said to be the one-stop rainforest experience on the other side of Kuala Lumpur. It includes nature trails, research centres, 'ethno-botanic' gardens, traditional houses, museums and a library. A compendium of Malaysian natural history, FRIM is part natural and part transplanted. The Sungei Kroh waterfall gurgles near an arboretum, a coniferatum, a bambusetum, and an insectorium among other nature repositories.

Five nature trails provide visitors with different rainforest experiences. Botanical species found here include the Kapur, Keladan, Gaharu, Merbau,

THIS PAGE (FROM TOP, LEFT): Mount Kinabalu is a popular hiking spot in Sabah; a bird's nest fern such as this can easily be spotted growing in trees; white water rafting is an adrenaline-pumping experience that can be enjoyed in Sabah's nature reserves.
OPPOSITE: Danum Valley is shrouded in mist in the early morning hours.

Engkabang and Rattan. Along the way, watch out for birds such as the crested serpent eagle and hornbills.

Right in the middle of urbanised Kuala Lumpur lies a primary rainforest retaining a surprisingly rich spread of flora. The **Bukit Nanas Forest Reserve** (Menara Kuala Lumpur, 2, Jalan Puncak) is a 10.5-hectare (25.9-acre) inner-city tropical rainforest located at the base of the 421-m- (1381-ft-) high KL Tower. Once part of a greater forest range which virtually canopied the entire stretch of the Peninsula, Bukit Nanas now stands as an anachronism within the concrete jungle. It also illustrates a vivid tableau in the enduring tussle between man and nature.

Only a hundred years back, tigers could be seen prowling near the hill, doubtlessly attracted to the bullocks that drew the carts carrying bricks and mortar for the construction of two local schools—St John's Institution and the Convent Bukit Nanas. Some species of flora found here include trees—Kapur, Keruing Bulu, Jelutong and Meranti Pa'ang—and rattan. Many of these specimens, especially along the marked-out trails, are helpfully tagged for the benefit of the casual trekker or nature enthusiast.

There are two prominent nature trails here—the 360-metre (1,181-ft) Merbau Trail and the 300-m (985-ft) Jelutong Trail. Look a little closer and you might just be able to spot gems of Malaysian flora such as the white-throated kingfisher, the yellow-vented bulbul, raucous macaques and playful silver leaf monkeys. For a trek through Bukit Nanas, it is best to begin one's journey bright and early at the base of the landmark KL Tower.

west malaysia

The natural landscape of Peninsular Malaysia can be as undulating as a green, roiling tide. Pristine shorelines give way to mangrove swamps, dense lowland forests and the jagged chain peaks of the Titiwangsa and Tahan mountain ranges. Such unmatched natural wealth places Malaysia among the top 12 'megabiodiversity' countries.

Parts of its shores beckon to the green and hawksbill turtles during their egg-laying seasons, while its estuaries still provide a haven to the critically endangered terrapins.

Lowland forests host more than 2,000 plant and tree species. The most eye-popping (and nose-twitching) one includes the world's largest flower, the Rafflesia. Whenever and wherever this parasitic plant blooms, its environs reek of a rotting cadaver.

Some species are discovered by pure accident. In February 2007, two environmentalists chanced upon an unusual orchid, which, later turned out to be the *Monomeria barbata*. It is far more common in the mountains of Nepal than it is in the tropics. This discovery was made in the Cameron Highlands, close to civilisation, and yet unnoticed till recently. Still, virgin green surrounds offer no guarantee against the dangers of extinction.

Around the same time, a research team from the National University of Singapore stumbled upon something that *The New York Times* subsequently described as 'looking like the plumbing on a rocket engine', or possibly 'an alpenhorn gone wild'. It turned out to be a unique snail species endemic only to the **Gunung Rapat** limestone karst near Ipoh, Perak.

Gunung Rapat regularly attracts another enduring breed—devotees and tourists to the **Sam Poh Tong temple cave complex**. Said to be the biggest cave temple in the country, it is an impressive work of art—various statues of Buddha are interspersed among the imposing stalactites and stalagmites. However, perhaps the most famous cave temple complex in Malaysia is the **Batu Caves**, located about 12 km (7.4 miles) north of Kuala Lumpur. A limestone hill, it consists of a network of caves and Hindu cave temples. During Thaipusam, the Batu Caves by themselves attract more than a million pilgrims.

While discoveries take place at a snail's pace, Mother Nature stoically waits to unveil secrets from her green treasure trove. Creatures only newly discovered, however, may very well disappear forever in the next fleeting moment. Some of them are, at the present, in danger of extinction.

The national coat of arms, the Jata Negara, is completed by two flanking tigers in the rampant position. In the wild, however, these magnificent beasts are more likely to adopt the couchant pose; waiting patiently for the day when their numbers exceed the present rounded figure of 500.

A committed coalition of NGOs and governmental bodies are working around the clock to resuscitate the *Panthera tigris jacksoni* subspecies to its former glory. Their habitat is now restricted to only four areas: **Royal Belum State Park**, the **Temenggor Lake** and surrounds, the Jeli district in Kelantan, in the northern part of the Peninsula, and the **Endau-Rompin district** to the south.

THIS PAGE (FROM TOP): A Sumatran rhinoceros grazes with her three-week-old female calf by her side; the Batu limestone caves are held sacred by many Hindu devotees.

OPPOSITE (FROM TOP, LEFT): Eco-tourists enjoy bird-watching—rare birds can be spotted in nature reserves such as the Taman Negara National Park; the odoriferous Rafflesia produces the largest flower in the world; a turtle laying its eggs in the sand.

nature

Conservationists who strive to protect the Malayan tiger, as well as the endangered Sumatran rhinoceros, often encounter other unique species during the course of their work. These include the Asiatic Elephant, leopards, tapirs and elusive pangolins as well as the giant Seladang.

Nature regularly plays hide-and-seek, and there are plenty of hidden nooks in which to play at this game in Peninsular Malaysia. From rare pitcher plants to giant insects to the crouching tiger, tracking any one of them can be daunting even for a trained biologist. For a tour de force of the peninsula's biodiversity, the **Taman Negara National Park** is the best one-stop destination. Here, one can fan out to explore the jungle, take a dip, ride on a boat, explore caves, clamber up a mountain and or simply chill beside a waterfall.

east malaysia

Borneo is the third largest island in the world, and perhaps the most bewildering in terms of biodiversity. Exceptionally dense forests, mountain ranges and the sea barrier have led to the evolution of a veritable cornucopia of tribal cultures and wildlife. Despite the relentless onslaught of modern-day industrial development and oil palm plantations, the East Malaysian states of Sabah and Sarawak, located on the northern swath of Borneo, still play host to some of the most unique species on earth.

This is where the geographical remoteness and a natural safe haven may have contributed to a curious downsizing of sorts among native elephants. The indigenous Borneo

pygmy elephant stands (not tall—but nonetheless still) proudly unique among its mammoth cousins, and is currently arousing a great deal of international interest.

However, if one needs to conjure up a symbol for Borneo, the native orangutan should rightfully claim that spot. This great ape, draped in distinctive reddish-brown hair, has a level of intelligence that is uncanny, even among primates. The orangutans' anthropomorphic affinity to humans is best encapsulated (some might say explained) by the literal translation of its name—'man of the forest'.

One of the best places to see a shaggy 100-kg (220 lb) Borneo orangutan up close in Sarakwak is **The Semenggoh Wildlife Rehabilitation Centre**. The apes roam freely around the forests surrounding the reserve and gather on the grounds of the centre during feeding sessions.

In Borneo, the orangutan reigns as the king of the jungle. Under this hierarchy are the Borneo clouded leopard, more than 220 species of mammals, close to 500 species of birds and 15,000 species of flowering plants and trees. According to one estimate, more than 360 new species were discovered in Borneo over the past 10 years. That translates to 36 species per year, or three species in one month. These flora and fauna can be found variously from lofty peaks to subterranean streams.

The highest peak in Malaysia is **Mount Kinabalu** in Sabah, towering at 4,095 m (13,435 ft) above sea level. It is an Everest in terms of biodiversity. It is home to more than 800 orchid and 600 fern species. All in all, there

are between 5,000 to 6,000 plant species along the base and slopes of this mountain, a staggering number breaching several world records.

Sarawak boasts its own world record. The **Gunung Mulu National Park** is a mountainous terrain covering some 52,000 hectares (128,495 acres) of primary rainforest, but its greatest treasure lies deep within a cavern—the **Mulu cave complex** is the largest and longest in the world, stretching over a whopping 200 km (124.3 miles). A significant portion of this limestone labyrinth remains unexplored. Some estimates place its unplumbed depths at as high as 70 per cent of its total.

THIS PAGE (FROM TOP): The 'Pinnacles' at the Gunung Mulu National Park; intrepid explorers in one of the caves of Gunung Mulu National Park.

OPPOSITE (FROM TOP, LEFT): Mount Kinabalu is Southeast Asia's highest mountain; carnivorous pitcher plants can be found in the tropical rainforests ; a rope bridge through the forest canopy caters for hikers and trekkers.

spas

Paradise is, it seems, accessible in Malaysia these days. Whether one is for a nifty urban pamper fest, or for a luxuriant beachfront spa holiday, the proliferation of well-considered, generally elegant spas throughout Malaysia makes this tropical haven the ideal candidate for a hedonistic holiday of the self-indulgent variety.

kuala lumpur

Spa Village Kuala Lumpur (Ritz-Carlton, Kuala Lumpur, 168 Jalan Imbi) is popular with the well-heeled and well-travelled, not least because the service there is consistently of a high standard. Throw in a mix of distinctive treatments and a setting that is designed to calm and regenerate, and it is little wonder that the spa took home the 2007 Urban Spa of the Year award. **Mandara Spa** is a familiar name amongst those who frequent spas, and its presence in various respected hotels across Kuala Lumpur, such as Prince Hotel & Residence Kuala Lumpur and Sunway Resort Hotel & Spa, is distinguished by the customised treatments on offer at each locale. Offering skin rejuvenating Decléor Facials and warm stone massages, the spa at

Prince Hotel & Residence Kuala Lumpur (Jalan Conlay) in the heart of the city is popular for a better-than-lunch pick-me-up. At the Sunway Resort Hotel & Spa across town (Persiaran Lagoon, Bandar Sunway), the signature Mandara massage incorporates Shiatsu, Thai, Hawaiian Lomi Lomi, Swedish and Balinese techniques, which, coupled with the resort's relatively recently completed Villas, make for a heady weekend getaway. The **Martha Tilaar Spa Eastern Rejuvenating Centre** (18th floor, Crown Princess Hotel, 182 Jalan Tun Razak) specialises in traditional Indonesian massages that are designed to improve virility and health and include signature treatments such as the lulur scrub and incense cleansing treatment. Around the corner at the Hotel Maya, the **Anggun Spa** (138 Jalan Ampang) offers a gamut of massage techniques—Malay urut, Shiatsu and Thai—to knead away boardroom-induced aches. The spa cuisine bar, serving healthy organic snacks and juices, will assist in the process of revitalisation. Fans of Malaysian jazz queen Sheila Majid will be enchanted by her Javanese-Balinese style **Jentayu Spa** (11 Jalan Gelanggang), where personalised service is one of the spa's signature flourishes. The Jentayu oil is the secret weapon of this intimate spa, and the sensual oil used in the Truly Heavenly Spa Treatment is said to be especially favoured by brides-to-be. Unisex expat-fave **Ozmosis** (1st floor , 14–16 Jalan Telawi 2, Bangsar Baru), which uses Dermalogica products, is a popular venue for pre- or post-prandial

treatments. But for a special no-holds-barred occasion, ask for the Ingrid Millet Perles de Caviar facial treat. The **Spa Indrani** (S27 Pamper Floor, Starhill Gallery, 181 Jalan Bukit Bintang) is frequented by discerning ladies who shop and adore the organic Ytsara spa range from Thailand and Phytomer marine spa products from France. But apart from the popular vinotherapy treatments available there, the spa's Talika eye ritual—touted to stimulate eyelash growth sans extensions or invasive treatments—is fast becoming the talk of the town. Living proof that gender-specific spas are on the ascent, the **Senjakala Urban Spa** (20 Jalan Pudu Lama) is a men's only haven that is ensconced in a colonial shophouse in the heart of the city. Senjakala means 'twilight', and the décor of its five dedicated levels is inspired by the dusky hues of sunset, whilst a range of treatments like the Tantric Discovery and Twilight Touch massage, which combines Swedish massage techniques with Thai and Malay flourishes, are testament to a burgeoning spa market amongst the urban Malaysian male.

west malaysia

Time-starved urbanites from Kuala Lumpur can now take a quick drive to Bukit Tinggi and the **Berjaya Hills Tatami Spa** (Colmar Tropicale, KM 48 Persimpangan Bertingkat, Lebuhraya Karak) for Japanese-inspired spa treatments and tranquillity. The first of its kind outside Japan, the tatami spa is surrounded by virgin rainforest and, at 1,066 m (3,500 ft) above sea level, the air there is bracingly fresh.

Present throughout the peninsula, the **Spa Village** brand is successful for its ability to reinvent itself: at the flagship spa in the **Pangkor Laut Resort** (Pangkor Laut Island, Lumut, Perak), the various healing cultures of the region are extolled and practised with alacrity, from Malay-style detoxifying and hydrating herbal wraps to Shanghainese scrubs. The Malay philosophy of suci murni or revival is celebrated at the **Tanjong Jara Resort** (Batu 8, off Jalan Dungun, Terengganu), and restorative Malay treatments are complemented by the skills of resident Malay healers for a complete holistic treatment. At the freshly refurbished wellness centre in **Cameron Highlands** (Cameron Highlands Resort, 39000 Tanah Rata, Pahang), treatments are inspired by indigenous tribal rituals of the jungle and draw upon the therapeutic qualities of the tea that is grown in plantations all around the highlands. The **Spa Village in The Majestic Malacca** (188 Jalan Bunga Raya) is the first and only spa worldwide to glean inspiration from the Baba-Nyonya or Peranakan culture. The unusual marriage of the Chinese and Malay cultures has yielded unique benefits such as the healing elements which have been incorporated into treatments at this spa. Further north, **The Spa at the Four Seasons Resort** in the idyllic island of Langkawi (Jalan Tanjung Rhu) is architecturally acclaimed, but the Ayurvedic treatments in the secluded and aesthetically pleasing pavilions are gaining momentum in their own right. One of the most beguiling features of the award-winning **Spa at the Datai**

(Jalan Teluk Datai, Langkawi) is a seamless integration of the treatment pavilions with the virgin rainforest into which the resort has been constructed. The **JivaRhu Spa** at Tanjung Rhu Resort (Mukim Ayer Hangat, Langkawi) draws its personality from the Sanskrit word 'jiva', literally meaning 'life'. Accordingly, the Malay-influenced spa treatments here are all designed to revive the five senses. At **The Spa at The Andaman Langkawi** (Jalan Teluk Datai), holistic spa treatments like the kerimi nut body polish and rose petal eye mask are given an added dimension by the eastern hospitality that accompanies each spa experience. Erstwhile The Westin Langkawi Resort & Spa's **Heavenly Spa** (Jalan Pantai Dato Syed Omar, Langkawi) is so special its name is trademarked. Its attendants are experts at customising treatments to individual needs.

On the Pearl of the Orient, Penang, **CHI, The Spa** at the Shangri-La Rasa Sayang Resort (Batu Ferringhi Beach, Penang) offers treatments that rebalance chakras, and the spa's holistic approach to well being incorporates ancient healing rituals from China and the Himalayas. The signature chi balance therapy treatment under century-old rain trees is an unforgettable experience.

east malaysia

Fast catching up with its peninsular cousin, there is no better testament to this than the East Malaysian **Mandara Spas** at **The Magellan Sutera** (1 Sutera Harbour Boulevard, Kota Kinabalu, Sabah), **The Pacific Sutera** (1 Sutera Harbour Boulevard, Kota Kinabalu, Sabah) and the

Miri Marriott Resort & Spa (Jalan Temenggong Datuk Oyong, Miri, Sarawak). The relatively new **Body Senses by Mandara** at The Pacific Sutera is geared towards the business traveller, and although the spa is simplicity defined, the attention paid towards each guest is far from spartan. In addition, multi-ethnic Miri is home to the signature Mandara massage at the Miri Marriott where two therapists use five different massage techniques to simultaneously revive mind and body. The **Borneo Spa** at the Nexus Resort Karambunai (off Jalan Sepangar Bay, Kota Kinabalu, Sabah) utilises time-tested Borneo philosophies of well-being in its spa therapy. The Borneo Massage—with its lymphatic acupressure techniques which detoxify the body whilst concurrently improving circulation, digestion and rebalancing emotions—is perennially popular.

THIS PAGE: A good facial helps blood circulation and eases wrinkles.
OPPOSITE: Enjoy a relaxing afternoon or evening with a stone therapy.
PAGE 66: KLCC Park in the city with Petronas Twin Towers in the background.

kualalumpur

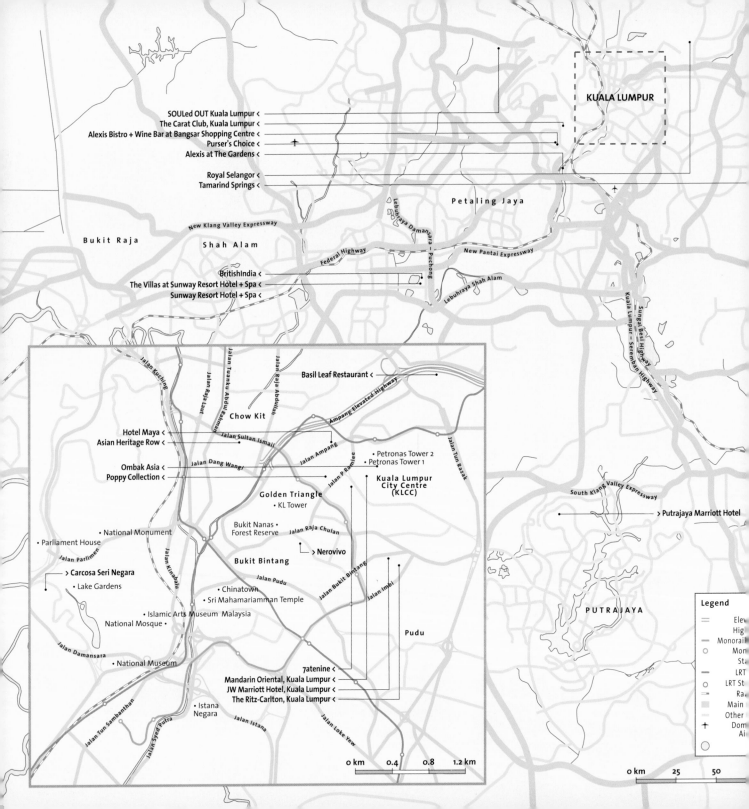

kuala lumpur

a tale of two cities

The name Kuala Lumpur is used freely to describe two different cities—KL and PJ (Petaling Jaya). The boundaries between the combined metropolises are sometimes so unclear, it can be hard to know which city one is in. 'Klang Valley' is a more accurate description of an entity that includes the adjacent townships of Shah Alam, Putrajaya, Cyberjaya and Klang. The abbreviation 'KV' has not, however, caught on.

KL is more than the capital of Malaysia, it is the centre of all major political, sporting and cultural activities. Among the most notable recent events was the comeback concert by Whitney Houston, which happened at the same riding club (Bukit Kiara Equestrian and Country Resort) where numerous equestrian world championships have taken place. KL's prominence is to some extent the result of 19th-century pragmatism, being halfway between Singapore and Penang, the Malay Peninsula's two main cities at the time. Singapore's Independence in 1965 gave greater prominence to KL, which took over many of the southern city's roles. These included establishing the *New Straits Times* in KL as Malaysia's official newspaper, leaving the long-established *Straits Times* based in Singapore.

KL is where most visits to Malaysia begin. The airport is large and well-organised; the links into the city are frequent and efficient. The city is smaller than most capitals and 20 years ago had almost no suburbs. Now the sprawl heads ever further in every direction. More than any city in the country, the hotels are excellent and reasonably priced. The most reassuring names in global hospitality are available, including Mandarin Oriental, Hyatt and Ritz-Carlton. The latest addition is Grand Millennium. There are some home-grown brands too, such as the Istana (which means 'palace' in Malay) and the Eastin.

Hotels are important. Social life revolves around them; for weekend dim sum, the family that eats together meets together at a hotel restaurant. Wedding dinners do not happen in Malibu-style gardens; any union which aims to make an impression will take place in a hotel, although entertainment superstars prefer to use convention centres so that they maximise guest attendance and media coverage. When politicians hold their annual so-called 'open houses', the venue is more likely to be a hotel function room than their own home. The importance of hotels is true of Malaysia as a whole, but in KL there is more choice. They provide venues for the finest dining and the most vibrant nightlife. 'Clubbing' is one of KL's most important after-hours pursuits, with the most salubrious clubs located in hotels. The same applies to restaurants.

THIS PAGE (FROM TOP): Kuala Lumpur International Airport is half an hour from the centre of the capital via rail link; this billboard consists of KL's two most prominent landmarks—the KL Tower and the Petronas Twin Towers.

PAGE 68: The Petronas Towers reflected in the windows of a nearby building.

The nation's capital has more than the greatest number and variety of hotels. It also houses most of the nation's premier urban attractions, and being a compact city, it is easy to move from one to another. The Petronas Twin Towers are a stone's throw from another high-rise tourist draw—the KL Tower. All the major shopping malls are in the same vicinity, providing a wide variety of bargain-hunting opportunities.

For most visitors, the excitement of the metropolis lies in imbibing its energy. The Chinatown and Masjid India neighbourhoods are living heritage sites of Malaysia's two leading minorities. They are especially vibrant before festivals such as Chinese New Year and Deepavali. For a glimpse of traditional Malay life there is a kampung situated in the heart of the city. Kampung Baru is a property developer's dream waiting to happen. In the meantime it retains the charm of the countryside, complete with houses on stilts and chickens that are so free range they have the run of the entire neighbourhood.

KL has also been improving its formal attractions. There is now a first-rate aquarium in KLCC, perhaps the only one in existence to use shards of Ming-dynasty ceramics in the fish tanks. The underwater park features 6,000 sq m (60,000 sq ft) with a 90-m (295-ft) long underwater tunnel, housing over 250 different species and over 20,000 land and aquatic animals from Malaysia and around the world. Being surrounded by a huge number of old shipwrecks gives Malaysia an additional allure for collectors in search of the past, although the dive sites are off limits to anyone but approved salvage specialists.

Nature still provides much of the charm of this very green city. This appeal is in abundance at the Lake Gardens, which have Malaysia's very modern parliament house at one end and a delightfully antiquated railway station at the other. Key sites are a butterfly park, an orchid garden, a hibiscus garden, a deer park and the Kuala Lumpur Bird Park, the world's largest

THIS PAGE: A view of the lit up Sultan Abdul Samad Building.

covered bird park. It is a joy simply to walk in this colonial-era sanctuary with its towering trees and legions of monkeys. The Malaysian National Monument, the world's largest freestanding bronze sculpture, can also be found within the park. Local picnickers are a common sight during the weekends. Joggers are a ubiquitous feature on any day of the week, but only in the early morning or evening.

Timing is everything in Kuala Lumpur. For pedestrians, it is the sun that matters. For motorists, it is the rush hour. The rain is something that everyone has to take into account. It tends to happen in the late afternoons and is as effective at stopping traffic as it is at ending a leisurely stroll. This accounts for much of the popularity of shopping malls, which now dominate city life. In the older neighbourhoods, it is still possible to admire the earlier solution—'five-foot ways'. These arcaded pavements originally provided shelter from the sun and rain but now represent the not so up-market side of shopping.

Kuala Lumpur is a city of contrasts. The old and the new sit side by side, with little interaction between the two. Visitors and expatriates get a chance to experience many aspects of Asia from a hundred years ago, including traditional artisans plying their trades, while enjoying the comforts of world-class hotels and shopping centres. It is the only city in Malaysia to have a light railway. This is really worth using, except during the rush hours.

The Petaling Jaya side of the city is less of a draw. Like much of the Klang Valley, it consisted of either plantations or tin mines until a few decades ago. For residents, it offers all the essentials of life, within a short commute of central KL. Many communities in KL and PJ have the feel of a village. Every neighbourhood has its own identity and they are not just dormitory towns for commuters. Commercial activity is spread throughout the Klang Valley, with large pockets of activity in areas that would be unlikely in London, Paris, New York or Tokyo.

KL provides a different sort of experience from most cities. Rapid growth has resulted in an essentially unplanned environment. It is a monument to freewheeling capitalism. The extremely light hand of government control has made this a fascinating environment in which the selfish side of humanity might be expected to predominate. Instead, it is a place where the inhabitants try harder than most to get on with their neighbours of different races, and to show more kindness to tourists than would be found in other capital cities of the world.

...get a chance to experience many aspects of Asia...

carcosa seri negara

Carcosa Seri Negara is a fairytale-styled boutique hotel, with two historic mansions cresting a beautifully landscaped hill above Kuala Lumpur's tropical Lake Gardens. With a heritage as sweeping and intricate as the development of modern-day Malaysia itself, Carcosa Seri Negara offers far more than a luxurious environment in which to escape the melee of the capital.

The story begins at the turn of the 20th century, when Kuala Lumpur was but a village and Sir Frank Swettenham was British advisor to the governing sultans. When Selangor, Perak, Pahang and Negiri Sembilan became a Federation, he became Resident General. He dammed a stream to create more public space with the verdant Lake Gardens, and commissioned a striking residence, Carcosa, overlooking the lake, as well as the adjacent King's House, which is known today as Seri Negara, or 'beautiful country' in Malay.

Now as then, Carcosa Seri Negara is the ultimate refuge for discerning travellers and statesmen. These two 'houses on the hill', protected by the Antiquities Act, are the perfect choice for private balls, formal receptions and romantic weddings. Though jolted into the present with the iconic silhouettes of the Petronas Twin Towers on the horizon, these havens retain the rarefied aura of their glamorous colonial past.

Carcosa boasts several private function rooms, as well as a spacious Marquee and The Dining Room, whose intimate ambience whispers untold tales of romance and mystery. The shaded Drawing Room verandah is a wonderful spot for an English cream tea, enjoyed against the colourful backdrop of the lush, manicured gardens.

In both mansions, each distinctive, air-conditioned suite offers satellite TV, a home theatre DVD and music system, and wireless Internet access. The grand Seri Ehsan and Seri Ridzuan terrace suites extend to almost 150 sq m (1,615 sq ft), with separate living and dining areas, walk-in wardrobes and sparkling, oversized bathrooms.

The immaculate Superior and Deluxe suites offer enclosed sun terraces to wrap-around balconies, many with panoramic views of the serene Lake Gardens. For those seeking extensive space, Seri Negara's largest suite, Seri Makmur, is the ideal choice. The suite features a jacuzzi and direct access to the Jerai function room.

For additional requests, a discreet butler is on hand 24 hours a day. It is personalised, no-expense-spared touches like this that really make Carcosa Seri Negara stand out. This stylish retreat never veers from its unstinting efforts to provide impeccable service and an unparalleled pampering experience to guests.

For excellent service and to experience the quintessence of colonial Malaysia with a uniquely modern twist, head for the seemingly untouched, privileged and elegant retreat that is Carcosa Seri Negara.

...the ultimate refuge for discerning travellers and statesmen.

rooms
13

food
The Dining Room: French • The Gulai House: traditional Malay

drink
The Drawing Room • The Bar

features
24-hour butler service • minibar • massage • home theatre system • wireless Internet access • limousine service

business
business centre • function rooms

nearby
Bukit Aman Mosque • KL Sentral • Bangsar Shopping Centre

contact
Taman Tasik Perdana, Persiaran Mahameru 50480 Kuala Lumpur •
telephone: +60.3.2295 0888 •
facsimile: +60.3.2282 7888 •
email: carcosa@ghmhotels.com •
website: www.ghmhotels.com

hotel maya

THIS PAGE: *The rooms at Hotel Maya are the height of contemporary chic.*

OPPOSITE (FROM TOP): *The Executive Suite will impress even the most discriminating dignitary; a striking arch of bamboo poles frames the soothing hydrotherapy pool.*

Malaysia has earned its fame in recent years for being one of the most formidable Asian tigers and, with its forest of skyscrapers, nowhere is this more evident than in Kuala Lumpur. A vibrant, multi-cultural community co-exists in this bustling capital, making for a fascinating mish-mash of cuisines, customs and architectures. Monuments of the scale of the Petronas Twin Towers dwarf quaint, colonial buildings, which in turn are juxtaposed against mosques and impeccably preserved cricket grounds.

Standing at the heart of the city's business and commercial districts, a short stroll away from the Suria KLCC shopping centre and the Petronas Twin Towers, Hotel Maya makes an ideal destination for visitors to Kuala Lumpur. A self-styled 'boutique urban resort', the hotel is a luxurious sanctuary encompassing everything a weary tourist or highly stressed business traveller might need.

The hotel stakes its individuality on the personal details that can really make a difference. Check-in can be as early as 7.00 am if need be and, instead of tiresome queues in the reception, it can be done in the comfort of one's room, accompanied by a soothing drink. A butler is on hand to help with the unpacking, giving guests a minute to soak up the breathtaking views of the city's skyline.

Hotel Maya's interiors are classically contemporary. The clear, simple lines of the furniture are echoed in the panelled, floor-to-ceiling windows, while woven screens and carved wood wall-cladding allude to Oriental architectural traditions. The spacious rooms are bathed in natural light and the intricate mosaic of the wooden floors create an atmosphere of warmth and elegance. Most rooms provide unobstructed views of either the KL Tower or the Petronas Twin Towers. Guests will be tempted to spend a quiet evening in, watching a movie from the in-house DVD selection before slumbering in a lavish, oversized bed with a selection of pillows to ensure a blissful night's sleep.

rooms
207

food
Still Waters: Sosaku • Maya Brasserie: international and Malay • Ramah Tamah: deli

drink
The Lobby Lounge • Sky Lounge

features
high speed Internet access • spa • hydrotherapy pool • gym • yoga classes • pilates classes • airport limousine service • business centre • conference facilities • spa cuisine

nearby
KLCC shopping centre • KL Tower • Petronas Twin Towers • Little India • Chinatown • Bukit Bintang

contact
138 Jalan Ampang, 50450 Kuala Lumpur • telephone: +60.3.2711 8866 • facsimile: +60.3.2711 9966 • email: info@hotelmaya.com.my • website: www.hotelmaya.com.my

Aware of the stresses that a city like Kuala Lumpur can inflict on the body and mind, Hotel Maya takes relaxation very seriously. A gym offering classes such as yoga and pilates makes a refreshing alternative, though water-babies will be tempted by the hydrotherapy pool which pummels the neck and shoulders with warm jets of water to literally wash away tension. The Anggun Spa completes the therapeutic experience, bringing together an array of massages that span the hotel's signature Malay Urut, Shiatsu and Thai, along with other revitalising and beautifying treatments.

Dining at Hotel Maya is as varied and cosmopolitan as the city itself, and will satisfy even the most discriminating of palates. The serene sophistication of Still Waters provides the perfect backdrop for fine dining. Ramah Tamah offers that ideal, light wholesome lunch or delectable cakes to accompany afternoon tea. Evenings can be enjoyed with a cocktail at the Sky Lounge, or authentic Malay cuisine from Maya Brasserie.

Be it for business or pleasure, staff at Hotel Maya understand exactly what it takes to create an experience that will ensure return visits time and time again.

jw marriott hotel kuala lumpur

THIS PAGE: The spacious Presidential Suite depicts style, luxury and modern comfort.

OPPOSITE (FROM TOP): Enjoy authentic Shanghainese fare at the Shanghai restaurant, which also serves dim sum and other Chinese dishes; the lobby inspires with its sophisticated décor.

Great for shoppers or for those in Kuala Lumpur for business, the elegant and luxurious JW Marriott Hotel Kuala Lumpur will ensure that a guest's stay in the capital is more than comfortable. The 29-storey five-star hotel, which opened its doors in 1997, is located at the Golden Triangle, the heart of Kuala Lumpur's business and shopping district.

Upon arrival, guests will immediately note the hotel's European flavour. With marble furnishings, wrought-iron filigree and a magnificent chandelier, a majestic air fills the lobby. Guestrooms are equally luxurious. Modern, yet have a touch of the old, classic dark wood furniture and plush carpets come as standards.

The business traveller will find these guestrooms a big plus. Large desks and an ergonomic leather chair will aid their daily tasks, while the rooms are also fitted with the latest communication devices, such as two-line telephones with voice mail, and fax and computer modem capabilities, which ensure that guests remain connected to the outside world at all times. The hotel has 47 meeting rooms, which are complemented by the business centre.

On the 24th floor is the JW Lounge, which can be accessed by Marriott Marquis Platinum and Gold Card members and guests staying in the suites and executive floors. The view at the top is spectacular—the Kuala Lumpur skyline, dominated by the luminous Petronas Twin Towers, is a sight to behold. And this view is sweetened by the complimentary breakfast, light refreshments or evening cocktails that are served to these special guests.

One of JW Marriott's appeals lies in its proximity to Starhill Gallery, which is just adjacent to the hotel. Considered one of the most sophisticated malls in Kuala Lumpur, Starhill Gallery is where the well-heeled shop. Trendy shops apart, guests also enjoy an impressive range of dining options in the mall. Most of these stylish restaurants—Shook!, Luk Yu Tea House and Fisherman's Cove—are found on the lower ground floor, aptly called the Feast Floor. To satisfy their sweet tooth, guests can also head to The

Lounge at Starhill, where they can sample English or Asian pastries and pies while lounging on comfy sofas.

Guests can also dine at Shanghai, the hotel's Chinese restaurant, which serves delectable Shanghainese cuisine. The Marriott Café by the poolside offers Western, international and Asian dishes. For pure indulgence, sample premium liqueurs and enjoy a cigar at Casa Havana, a bar where one can chill out and fantasise about old world Havana. At the end of the day, the Starhill Spa, with its extensive range of treatments, is the ideal place to stop by for a rejuvenating spa session.

Impeccable service, great dining options and a perfect location—JW Marriott Hotel is the obvious choice for the discerning traveller looking for a luxurious stay in Kuala Lumpur.

rooms
561

food
Marriott Café: local and international • Shanghai: Shanghainese

drink
The Lounge at Starhill

features
grand ballroom • banquet rooms • spa • gym • relaxation lounges • aerobics room • sauna • tennis court • plunge pool • outdoor pool

business
business centre

nearby
Bintang Walk • Starhill Gallery • Lot 10 Shopping Centre

contact
183 Jalan Bukit Bintang, 55100 Kuala Lumpur • telephone: +60.3.2715 9000 • facsimile: +60.3.2715 7000 • email: jwmh@po.jaring.my • website: www.ytlhotels.com.my/ properties/jwmarriot

mandarin oriental, kuala lumpur

THIS PAGE: *Cool off by the infinity-edge pool while gazing at the lush greenery of KLCC Park.*
OPPOSITE (FROM TOP): *Premium rooms with stunning views of the Petronas Twin Towers are perennial guest favourites; dine in comfort with the lights of the city as backdrop.*

One of Mandarin Oriental Hotel Group's missions is to 'completely delight and satisfy guests', and this they do day after day at their magnificent property in Kuala Lumpur. The hotel is located at the very heart of the capital, forming an integral part of the Kuala Lumpur City Centre (KLCC), a residential, commercial, business and entertainment district focused around the imposing Petronas Twin Towers. Standing before a lush 20-hectare (50-acre) park, with sweeping views of the city's changing skyline, the award-winning Mandarin Oriental, Kuala Lumpur is the first choice of discerning business and leisure travellers.

The hotel is a stunning combination of classical, contemporary design infused with traditional influences, for an effect that is sophisticated and luxurious. The majestic stage is set by the lobby's decorative black and tangerine marble floor, while a fresh yet elegant atmosphere pervades in the lounge area, where the furnishings are accented with deep blues and ochres. The rooms with panoramic windows are bedecked in glimmering silks exuding warmth and comfort. All rooms come with high-speed Internet access, dual phone lines and deep, marble bathtubs for that long, hot soak to wash away the stresses of the day. The Mandarin Oriental Club, occupying the

rooms
643

food
Pacifica Grill & Bar: international • Lai Po Heen: Cantonese • Wasabi: Californian-Japanese • Biba's Café: international and regional • Cascade Restaurant & Bar: Mediterranean

drink
Lounge on the Park

features
high-speed Internet access • spa • satellite TV • tennis courts • squash courts • cigar divan • Mandarin Oriental Club

business
conference facilities • business centre

nearby
KLCC park • Suria KLCC shopping centre • Aquaria KLCC • Petronas Twin Towers • KL Convention Centre

contact
Kuala Lumpur City Centre PO Box 10905, 50088 Kuala Lumpur • telephone: +60.3.2380 8888 • facsimile: +60.3.2380 8833 • email: mokul-sales@mohg.com • website: www.mandarinoriental.com

24th to 30th floors of the hotel, will especially delight business travellers. Guests staying at the Club floors benefit from complimentary use of the Club Lounge (including a billiard and computer room), access to the Executive Business Centre and complimentary laundry, dry-cleaning and pressing service.

If unwinding is high on the list of priorities, Mandarin Oriental will not disappoint. Those looking for a workout can choose from the myriad of options offered at the Vitality Club. Guests can swim in the infinity-edge pool, play a game of tennis, work out in the gym, or attend an aerobics, kick-boxing or yoga class. Those looking for something less rigorous can indulge at The Spa at Mandarin Oriental, where ancient Malay, Thai and Chinese therapies are offered.

Dining at Mandarin Oriental is as scintillating and diverse as the city of Kuala Lumpur. Showcasing an innovative fusion of contemporary European cuisine with Asian influences in a colourful, eclectic ambience is the Pacifica Grill & Bar. The exquisitely decorated Lai Po Heen restaurant serves traditional Cantonese delicacies and an irresistible array of dim sum, while Wasabi Bistro specialises in nouvelle Californian-Japanese cuisine featuring fresh seafood.

Mandarin Oriental, Kuala Lumpur, with everything it has to offer, certainly fulfils its mission to completely delight and satisfy guests. In fact, the hotel does not merely delight and satisfy, it goes beyond that to completely exceed expectations.

putrajaya marriott hotel

The Putrajaya Marriott is a massive, majestic and Moorish-themed castle of a hotel. With swaying palm trees and a Mediterranean feel, it is all the more eye-catching for being slightly architecturally anachronistic.

The lobby alone makes a striking impression. Covering a vast 1 hectare (2.5 acres) of space, it is dominated by cascading water fountains and intricately corniced high ceilings. Beyond this lie 380 spacious guestrooms, 35 suites and 73 executive rooms, housed on their own concierge floor. These en-suite havens come with IDD phones, satellite TV and Internet access. To unwind after a long day's work or play, slip into the deep soaking tub or enjoy a rejuvenating shower in the gleaming private bathroom.

The Putrajaya Marriott has a state-of-the-art fitness centre, a holistic spa and sauna, and extensive massage options. The outdoor pool comes complete with its own tropical pool bar, Splash. There is also a 27-hole championship golf course. Foodies will be in seventh heaven here. Summer Palace offers Szechuan and Cantonese cuisine, while Midori serves sushi and sashimi. For a Mediterranean feel, head to the Italian restaurant Tuscany. Local and international delicacies can be had at The Terrace Café, while the sophisticated Lobby Lounge is the perfect place for wine and cocktails.

For special events, the Putrajaya Marriott guarantees a flawless experience. The Grand Ballroom, resplendent in majestic golden and vivid red drapes, is the largest pillar-less ballroom in the region. Perfect for product launches or conferences, it accommodates up to 1,500 people beneath the impressive domes of its corniced ceiling. There are also 22 smaller meeting rooms to choose from.

Not merely a luxurious business-savvy resort but a magnet for sun-lovers and discerning leisure travellers, the Putrajaya Marriott has many sides to its impressive personality. Get to know them all with a sojourn at this masterpiece of a hotel.

...a magnet for sun-lovers and discerning leisure travellers...

rooms
488

food
Summer Palace: Szechuan and Cantonese •
Midori: Japanese • Tuscany: Italian •
Terrace Café: local and international

drink
Lobby Lounge • Splash pool bar

features
satellite TV • high-speed Internet access

business
business centre • conference facilities

nearby
Kuala Lumpur • KL International Airport •
Sepang International Circuit • Putra Mosque •
Perdana Putra • Alamanda shopping mall •
lakes and wetlands

contact
Putrajaya Marriott Hotel IOI Resort
62502 Putrajaya
telephone: +60.3.8949 8888 •
facsimile: +60.3.8949 8999 •
email: sales.hotel@marriottputrajaya.com •
website: www.marriott.com/kulpg

sunway resort hotel + spa

Certain resorts offer certain things to some people. Kuala Lumpur's landmark Sunway Lagoon Resort aims to offer practically all things to everyone with its fully integrated leisure, business and five-star resort complex.

This destination of spectacular choices has become one of Malaysia's most iconic developments. A 324-hectare (800-acre) 'resort within the city', its diverse guestrooms are complemented by a state-of-the-art business centre and a boutique-lined mall, among other attractions. Recreational opportunities also abound, with a Balinese-inspired spa, 24-hour fitness centre and a jogging track.

In addition, Sunway Lagoon Resort offers an adventure in dining, with its wide array of fine food and drink venues. From contemporary Italian-American cuisine—accompanied by a melodious piano singer—to high tea at the Sun and Surf Café, there is a restaurant to suit every occasion and culinary persuasion, from Cantonese and Korean to vibrant bars with pool tables and live bands.

The flagship hotel at this new generation complex is the five-star Sunway Resort Hotel & Spa. Its modern guestrooms include tastefully furnished suites, with select suites authentically themed Arabian, Tranquillity and Hollywood. On the other hand, The Club takes the on-the-go lifestyle to an entirely new level. The new category of Premier Rooms additionally captures the urban vibrancy of Sunway Resort Hotel & Spa, whether enjoyed for one restful night or a hectic week.

Other impeccably appointed guestrooms are located within the striking Pyramid Tower Hotel. Guests can also opt for the hotel's collection of chic, home-from-home studios that are ideal for longer sojourns. For travellers seeking spacious accommodation, The Duplex

...fully integrated leisure, business and five-star resort complex.

rooms
1,234

food
Avanti Italian American Ristorante: Italian and American • Sun and Surf Café: international • West Lake Garden: Cantonese • KoRyo-Won: Korean • Atrium Café: pan-Asian

drink
The Lobby Lounge • Atrium Lounge

features
Internet • satellite TV • minibar • pool • jogging track • fitness centre • spa • shuttle service • limousine

nearby
Sunway Lagoon Theme Park • Sunway Pyramid Shopping Mall • Euphoria Kuala Lumpur by Ministry of Sound • Kuala Lumpur City Centre

contact
Persiaran Lagoon, Bandar Sunway 46150 Petaling Jaya, Selangor Darul Ehsan • telephone: +60.3.7492 8000 • facsimile: +60.3.7492 8001 • email: enquirysrhs@sunwayhotels.com • website: www.sunwayhotels.com

boasts 12 private townhomes, which have access to full hotel services, from housekeeping to laundry and pressing. Sunway Resort Hotel & Spa also offers a unique alternative with The Villas, 17 tailor-made, Asian-styled masterpieces that are the first of their kind in Kuala Lumpur and perfectly tailored for tranquillity and relaxation.

Even with the option to indulge in the world-class Mandara Spa or frolic in the waters of the free-form pool with its cascading fountains, there are some for whom a hotel room's electronic gadgetry will always hold a childlike fascination. Each Sunway Resort Hotel & Spa guestroom is fully-equipped with high-speed Internet access, satellite TV, movie channels and a fully stocked minibar. This makes it a veritable den of modern comforts for those who prefer to stay in and relax after a strenuous day-trip or long haul flight.

Indeed, Sunway Resort Hotel & Spa lays myriad possibilities on the table, and it is up to each guest to choose which experiential cards they would like to turn over.

the ritz-carlton, kuala lumpur

THIS PAGE: *Li Yen serves delectable Cantonese fare in a luxurious setting.*

OPPOSITE (FROM TOP): *The hotel's full butler service is available in guestrooms and suites alike; enjoy a drink and relax in the tropical environs of the pool.*

When The Ritz-Carlton, Kuala Lumpur opened its doors in 1997, its 19th-century English-styled guestrooms exuded warmth and an old world charm, sprinkling some European flavour in the middle of Kuala Lumpur's busy Golden Triangle, the Malaysian capital's shopper's haven. The five-star hotel has since undergone a revamp. It recently refreshed its look to reflect Malaysia's unique ethnic and artistic heritage as well. The hotel's interiors can now be described as 'European elegance meets Asian sensibilities.'

Made of rich, dark wood, the furniture in the guestrooms adds to the cosy ambience, complemented by the soft and neutral tones of the walls. For ultimate comfort, look no further than the feather bed with its silky bed sheets and soft pillows.

While the hotel has an elegant and contemporary feel to it, it maintains a warm and welcoming atmosphere as well. To make their stay even more comfortable, guests can call on the hotel's butler service anytime, be it to serve them breakfast, or fill the bath.

rooms
365

food
Rossini's: creative morning cuisine • Li Yen: Cantonese • The Lobby Lounge: local and Western • Carlton Gourmet: delicatessen

drink
The Lobby Lounge

features
high-speed Internet access • butler service • flat-screen TV • rainforest showerheads • Spa Village • sauna • steam room •jacuzzi • 24-hour fitness centre

business
conference centre • business centre • conference concierge • secretarial services

nearby
Starhill Gallery • Bintang Walk • Bukit Bintang

contact
168 Jalan Imbi, 55100 Kuala Lumpur • telephone: +60.3.2142 8000 • facsimile: +60.3.2143 8080 • email: ritzkl@ritzcarlton.com.my • website: www.ritzcarlton.com

Tea lovers can ensconce themselves in the comfortable surroundings of the Lobby Lounge. There are an amazing 40 tea flavours to choose from, which guests can enjoy with freshly baked scones, chocolate lavender biscuits and delicious pastries.

And since the hotel is located next to Starhill Gallery, Malaysia's Fifth Avenue, there are numerous places to dine at. The Feast Village, in particular, offers an impressive range of fine dining options. Alternatively, there's Ritz-Carlton's Chinese restaurant, Li Yen, which means 'beautiful garden' in Chinese. Here, guests can enjoy Cantonese cuisine while listening to live traditional Chinese music from the yangqin—Chinese hammered dulcimer—in the evenings.

On the fourth floor is the 1,115-sq-m (12,000-sq-ft) Spa Village that offers a wide range of indulgent treatments and facilities including outdoor showers, sunken baths surrounded by tropical greenery, a lap pool, hot spa and cool dipping pool. The sensory room, which provides vibrating sensations designed to soothe and heal, is the first of its kind in the region. Outside the Spa Village, the hotel's pool, fringed by lush palms and tropical plants, is also an ideal spot for some contemplation and exercise.

With a strategic location right in the heart of the bustling capital, the hotel is a favourite among business travellers and holidaymakers alike. And at The Ritz-Carlton, Kuala Lumpur, business is pleasurable indeed.

the villas at sunway resort hotel + spa

The Villas at Sunway Resort Hotel & Spa is Kuala Lumpur's very first full-service villa accommodation, carefully dotted within a 324-hectare (800-acre) sanctuary of modern luxury and convenience.

This exclusive haven of tranquillity is the pièce de résistance of the iconic Sunway Resort Hotel & Spa, which offers various types of accommodation. There are hotels, stylish townhomes and the like, which are complemented by the Balinese Mandara Spa, theme parks and high-end shopping opportunities. Perfect for those seeking a distinct and inspiring holiday experience, the 17 Asian-inspired villas are ideal for peace and relaxation. Here, one can escape the quotidian, slip into anonymity or celebrate a special occasion in true style.

With full access to the resort's five-star facilities, The Villas offers the best of both worlds. Guests can either visit The Pavillion, exclusively for those staying at The Villas, the Hotel's vibrant bars, cosy lounges or restaurants to satiate their culinary desires,

THIS PAGE (FROM TOP): The private plunge pool is ideal for a relaxing dip; neutral and soft colour tones give suites a cosy atmosphere.

OPPOSITE (FROM LEFT): Guests can look forward to a rejuvenating floral bath; each villa features a private balcony that is perfect for sipping a cocktail over sunset.

Each villa is a personalised cocoon of calm.

or simply arrange private, in-villa dining. The Pavillion also caters for savouring a favourite snack or cocktail, music, cigar or more.

Each villa is a personalised cocoon of calm. An indulgent sense of space is engendered by the lofty, high-beamed ceiling and gleaming wooden floors. The soothing vanilla walls provide a neutral backdrop for the fine furnishings and details that make the property unique. Harmoniously fusing stylish interiors with nature-inspired, exotic exteriors, these charming villas provide the sought-after key to a world of laid-back tropical luxury. These masterpieces of Asian interior design boast exclusive use of an alluring infinity-edge plunge pool. Warmed by the

sun and surrounded by beckoning deck chairs from which to soak up the colourful surrounds and unhurried atmosphere, midnight dips come highly recommended.

The Villas' generous, sunken baths are temptation personified, with a range of fresh, botanic ingredients and heavenly scented essential oils just waiting to ease away the troubles of the day. For more dedicated relaxation, the award-winning Mandara Spa at Sunway Resort Hotel & Spa offers an eclectic menu of spa treatments, designed to elevate the body, mind and spirit to a state of inner peace. Experience a wrap, facial, invigorating scrub or uplifting massage in one of its 10 sumptuous spa suites, each enhanced by Balinese elements.

The impeccably appointed Villas at Sunway Resort Hotel & Spa are equipped to the same exacting standards as the executive suites in Sunway's flagship hotel. Whether guests are staying just for a night or planning a longer stopover, they may avail themselves of satellite TV, movie channels and a fully stocked minibar. As a good night's sleep is an essential element of any stay, oversized beds romantically draped in sheer fabrics are de rigueur. In addition, The Villas' guests may take advantage of a discreet butler service that will ensure every whim and request is fulfilled, no matter how small.

Guests will find themselves more than happy to exchange the limitations of daily life for the luxuries of a stay at The Villas and the experience of a memorable Asian getaway.

rooms
17 villas

food
The Pavillion: speciality cuisine

drink
extensive wine list

features
private plunge pool • satellite TV • minibar • spa • fitness centre • butler service

nearby
Sunway Pyramid Shopping Mall • Euphoria Kuala Lumpur by Ministry of Sound • Kuala Lumpur City Centre

contact
Persiaran Lagoon, Bandar Sunway 46150 Petaling Jaya, Selangor Darul Ehsan • telephone: +60.3.7495 1646 • facsimile: +60.3.7492 8007 • email: thevillas@sunwayhotels.com • website: www.sunwayhotels.com

7atenine

Kuala Lumpur offers a vast and ever-shifting array of drinking, culinary and live music establishments. To discover a sophisticated venue that weaves all three together in one exclusive dining and chill out venue, head to the unique 7atenine. An avant-garde interior and a dynamic atmosphere give 7atenine a contemporary feel, and with a reservation list resembling the Who's Who of Malaysian society, it is no wonder its tagline proclaims, 'you never know who you'll meet!'.

There is a play on words behind this unusually named destination, which won the 'Chill Out Bar of the Year' award at the 2007 Hospitality Asia Platinum Awards. Seven is the number of like-minded people responsible for its conception and evolution.

Nine reflects its address at the luxurious Ascott Residences. 'Ate' simply because the team enjoys puns as much as it revels in providing cosmopolitan cuisine and world-class musical experiences for its guests. Seven, ate, nine.

Providing welcome respite from the metropolis outside, 7atenine offers a multi-sensory dining experience across two floors of palate-pleasing innovation. The ground floor offers Scrumptious Seven nibbles and gourmet pizza. For more refined Western and Asian fare, ascend to the striking mezzanine to survey the scene below.

Culinary and cocktail creativity is at the heart of 7atenine's philosophy. Talented Resident Chef Patrick McHugh inspires with

THIS PAGE (FROM LEFT): 7atenine exudes a sophisticated charm; the trendy restaurant and its bar attract music and food connoisseurs alike.

OPPOSITE (FROM TOP): White dominates 7atenine's organic colour scheme, providing it with a clean and stylish look; delectable fare awaits guests.

...multi-sensory dining experience across two floors of palate-pleasing innovation.

seats
200

food
gourmet pizza • Scrumptious Seven nibbles • tasting platters • Asian • Western

drink
exclusive 7atenine cocktails • extensive wine list

features
extensive live music line-up • wireless Internet • painted fringe artists mingling with the crowd

nearby
Kuala Lumpur City Centre

contact
Ascott Kuala Lumpur 9
Jalan Pinang, 50450 Kuala Lumpur •
telephone: +60.3.2161 7789 •
facsimile: +60.3.2163 7789 •
email: ask@sevenatenine.com •
website: www.sevenatenine.com

his innovative global dishes, which use the freshest ingredients and artful presentation techniques. Bar maestros will conjure up their very own haute couture creations, from Chic-tinis like Nights in White Satin to the mouthwatering Coming Up Roses.

When it comes to lounge music and entertainment, 7atenine has a live music line-up to die for and, indeed, to dine for. Recent star performers include Nana (Asia's answer to Aretha Franklin), top French DJ Gregoire and the internationally renowned guitarist Jaime Wilson. Every musical taste is catered for, from mainstream jazz and funk to soul, hip-hop and rhythm and blues. On a daily basis, 7atenine plays eclectic international music within the range of electro, funk, jazz, soulful Latin and vocal house. Diamonds + Pearls, held on Saturdays, will make partygoers' night out an even more sublime experience. This theme night features a cast of DJs, predominantly of the fairer sex, spinning diverse sounds that complement 7atenine's chic selection of tunes.

Refurbished for its grand opening in 2006, 7atenine's design is the brainchild of Ed Poole, an intuitive interior designer whose work has been featured in *Time* and *Wallpaper*. Intimate, cosy and with an emphasis on relaxed elegance, 7atenine has a diverse clientele, from hip locals to discerning travellers, of which there is always room for one more.

alexis at the gardens

THIS PAGE: After a long day at the office, drop by Alexis @ The Gardens and order a drink from the bar.

OPPOSITE (FROM TOP): The minimalist décor lends an atmosphere of relaxed elegance to the restaurant; Alexis is known both for its stylish ambience and its superb food.

The Alexis chain's newest outlet is located at The Gardens, the new high-end, boutique shopping extension to Mid Valley Megamall. Despite a very low-key opening, Alexis @ The Gardens is quickly gaining a reputation for intimate yet elegant dining. Positioned in a discreet corner of the mall, the restaurant is fast becoming a magnet for both shoppers and professionals seeking refreshment.

While Alexis @ The Garden's menu shares some similarity with that of other outlets, the restaurant is noteworthy for its tapas kitchen, which offers pleasant surprises such as lightly fried calamari rings, carpaccio of yellowtail and tiger prawns in chilli-infused extra virgin olive oil.

Alexis restaurants are known for their excellent pizza, and Alexis @ The Gardens certainly does not disappoint. Its gamberetto of garlic prawns, oven-dried tomatoes and rocket leaves particularly stand out. One must also sample the Salad Niçoise, which consists of seared sashimi tuna, haricot vert, kalamata olives and soft-boiled egg. Only the freshest ingredients are used, ensuring a truly satisfying meal.

seats
restaurant and bar: 120 • private dining room: 16 • Cellars: 18

food
Asian • Western • pasta • pizza • tapas

drink
extensive wine list • cocktails

features
bar • private dining room • Cellars

nearby
Mid Valley Megamall

contact
Lot F209, 1st floor, The Gardens
Mid Valley City, Lingkaran Syed Putra
59200 Kuala Lumpur •
telephone: +60.3.2287 2281 •
email: info@alexis.com.my •
website: www.alexis.com.my

The crowning glory of the outlet, however, is its Wagyu beef dishes. It is questionable whether any other restaurant in Malaysia serves Wagyu beef cheeks or rib-eye steak straight from the grill in a more refined and delicious manner. The Chicken Escalope and Slow Roast Duck Breast are also joys to behold and divine to taste, even if one is not partial to these types of meat. There is a good selection of desserts to choose from, in particular the assorted cakes, which go down particularly well with ice-cream.

The ambience is cool and contemporary. While Alexis @ The Gardens interior evokes the same minimalist, unfinished feel of its sister outlets, the restaurant is completely at home in the opulent surroundings of The Gardens. The parquet floor of the main dining area gives way to the terrazzo finish of the bar, while the grey-on-white furnishings are complemented nicely by the adjustable lighting. With 120 seats, Alexis @ The Gardens is by far the largest Alexis restaurant. There is also a private dining room that seats 16 guests. However, absolute privacy, is to be had in the reservations-only Cellars, which can accommodate 18 guests. The entire Alexis Group's fine wine collection is stored in this room.

The restaurant is open for lunch and dinner daily, though only pizza and tapas are served from 10.00 pm onwards. Offering good food and excellent wine in luxurious surroundings, Alexis @ The Gardens is everything a discerning shopper or gourmand could ask for in a dining establishment.

alexis bistro + wine bar at bangsar shopping centre

THIS PAGE: Dine in comfort at the stylish Alexis BSC.

OPPOSITE (FROM TOP): The restaurant's extensive wine collection lines the shelves, forming a stark contrast to the white furnishings; a mouthwatering dish.

Like its venerable shopping mall host, Alexis Bistro & Wine Bar @ Bangsar Shopping Centre (Alexis BSC) has long been an established haunt for the gilded youth of Kuala Lumpur, as well as the city's well-established expatriate community. While it is not the largest or oldest member of the Alexis chain, the restaurant's location gives it a certain cachet that its sister establishments can only envy.

Open for breakfast, lunch and dinner every day, Alexis BSC offers an eclectic mix of Eastern and Western culinary delights. However, the place is not some experimental 'fusion' joint or anything of that sort. Rather, the restaurant is a solid eatery offering the best food and wine from around the world.

Tucked away in a discreet corner of Bangsar Shopping Centre, Alexis BSC boasts a minimalist white interior that is both soft and pleasing to the eye. The fact that the restaurant's lighting can be adjusted at any time to guests' specifications only heightens the cosiness and intimacy of the surroundings.

The restaurant's signature dish is the Sarawak Laksa—noodle soup served with chicken, prawns and bean sprouts. It is a relatively mild version of a perennial favourite, but nevertheless still a flavourful offering which is guaranteed to tantalise the taste buds. Alexis BSC is also known for its thin-crust pizza. Those who have sampled the Ai Frutti di Mare, with its combination of seafood, tomatoes and fresh herbs, could not praise it highly enough.

Another recommended dish is the Boeuf Bourguignon, a hearty stew with generous helpings of mashed potato and vegetables. The Alexis Club Sandwich is also a must-try, along with any salad on the menu. For

seats
restaurant: 90 • private dining room: 20

food
Asian • Western • pasta • pizza

drink
extensive wine list • cocktails

features
bar • private dining room • condiments rack

nearby
Alexis Bangsar • bistros • bars

contact
Lot F15A, 1st floor, Bangsar Shopping Centre
285 Jalan Maarof, Bukit Bandar Raya
59000 Kuala Lumpur •
telephone: +60.3.2287 1388 •
email: info@alexis.com.my •
website: www.alexis.com.my

dessert, diners can try the tiramisu and the Pavlova. The caramelized nut toppings of the tiramisu and the wild berries in the Pavlova promise a satisfying end to an already excellent dinner.

After a hearty meal, linger for a little while longer and order wine from the bar. Alexis BSC's French wines are of the finest vintage, and they are imported directly by Alexis Group, the chain's holding company. There is also New World selection, with wine from Oceania, South Africa and the Americas. An extensive range of champagne, cocktails and mocktails is available as well, along with coffee for non-drinkers.

Alexis BSC boasts a well-stocked condiments rack, with delights such as Simon Johnson olive oil and pasta sold on retail, along with most of the wines produced by the Australian food company.

The restaurant comfortably seats 80–90 guests. There is also a private dining room that can accommodate 20 people. For parties, Alexis BSC can install partitioning screens for added privacy.

Indeed, Alexis BSC is an ideal place to relax after a busy day of shopping at one of Malaysia's most enduring malls, or to simply see and be seen in Bangsar, a favourite hang-out of the young and upwardly mobile.

asian heritage row

THIS PAGE (FROM TOP): *The atmosphere at Cynna is intimate and sensual; deep shades of red dominate W Wine Room's décor.*

OPPOSITE (FROM TOP): *Its black, gold and white interior lends opulence to Heritage Mansion; Asian Heritage Row at night.*

While Kuala Lumpur has always had a superb reputation for its food, it has tended to lag behind other great capital cities in terms of the more stylish aspects involved in its consumption. However, all that has changed with the opening of Asian Heritage Row, a major redevelopment in the quaint quarter of Jalan Doraisamy. At last, Kuala Lumpur has a fashionable district that can hold its own with the likes of Montmartre in Paris, Soho in New York, Lan Kwai Fong in Hong Kong and Clark Quay in Singapore.

Conveniently located in the heart of the city, just off Jalan Sultan Ismail and close to the Imperial Hotel, Asian Heritage Row encompasses a row of 80-year-old prewar houses—long abandoned and ignored—that have been sympathetically restored as a series of hip establishments, transforming the neighbourhood into one of the most diverse and exciting in the Far East.

There is certainly no lack of choice at Asian Heritage Row. A cursory glance at the list of establishments in the area reveals enough choices to satisfy even the most varied of tastes. Restaurants featuring almost every major cuisine on the planet are represented. Those hoping to enjoy a drink will not be disappointed, either. Wine bars, lounge bars, jazz bars and cafés offer plenty

...a hive of dynamic activity.

food
Heritage Mansion: international • CoChine Lounge & Restaurant Bar SaVanh: Indochinese • Bisou: cakes and pastries • Kristao: Malaccan-Portuguese • Senja Bistro: Malay • The Ivy: classic English • Mezza Notte@The Loft: Italian and Japanese • Palacio: French and Spanish • Buharry Bistro: Malaysian

drink
Heritage Mansion • W Wine Room • Sunshine Classic Bar • The Rupee Room • barBlonde • Mojo • The Loft KL • Upstairs@The Loft • Cynna@The Loft • Bed • Atrium • Bar Club • Maison

features
restaurants • cafés • bars • clubs • lounges

nearby
Imperial Hotel

contact
11-01 Heritage House, 33 Jalan Yap Ah Shak 50300 Kuala Lumpur • telephone: +60.3.2694 6460 or +60.3.2694 6462 • facsimile: +60.3.2694 6682 • email: enquiry@asianheritagerow.com • website: www.asianheritagerow.com

of options both in terms of the products on offer and the fashionable environments in which to savour them.

For those in search of a little late night entertainment, there are plenty of nightclubs as well. Perhaps the most individually striking of these is the Asian Heritage Mansion—far and away the most exciting club to ever open in Kuala Lumpur. The anchor establishment at Heritage Avenue, this club—which also doubles as a dining parlour and funky café— is exclusively by invitation only. Centred round its legendary Fashion Bar, Heritage Mansion is the chosen playground of the city's elite and international jetsetters alike. Crowds do not come any hipper and trendier than the beautiful people who flock to this place, and A-list types hoping to enjoy clubbing at its most vibrant would be well advised to check the scene out. Enjoy occasional live band performances, ogle stunning men and women during Wednesday Models Night Fashion Express, and dance the night away on DiscoLicious Thursdays. Groove to house music on Fridays and Saturdays, and enjoy a carefree afternoon during Sunday Barbeque.

Indeed, the current Asian Heritage Row is a hive of dynamic activity. And this fine dining, nightlife and entertainment strip will only get more exciting, with the planned addition of upmarket fashion outlets, beauty salons and an art gallery on Heritage Avenue, in Jalan Kamunting. Soon, the place will be transformed into a complete lifestyle village, where one can not only enjoy superb food and wine, hang out and people-watch, but also go shopping in a number of chic establishments. When that happens, Asian Heritage Row will truly be a destination to rival the best that the rest of the world has to offer.

basil leaf restaurant

Kuala Lumpur offers a smorgasbord of culinary diversions. From unique local delicacies served at the roadside to world-class European, Pacific-fusion and Indian cuisine offered at stylish restaurants, this endlessly innovative city has it all. There is, however, only one place to go for an authentic Indochinese encounter, and that is Basil Leaf Restaurant.

Entry is via a pleasant curved walkway, tickled by tropical fronds and swaying bamboo. This natural corridor leads to a comfortable garden patio, where the friendly staff will happily serve a refreshing glass of lemon-grass juice and usher guests into the restaurant or to an outdoor terrace table.

Offering a complete dining experience, Basil Leaf aims to indulge all five senses simultaneously. The initial impression is one of a cosmopolitan restaurant, popular with local patrons as well as a well-travelled international clientele. Striking ebony chairs gleam against softly lit walls, which are themselves informed by passionate tones of scarlet and fuchsia. Fingertips are drawn to trace the outlines of the flowing Eastern and modern sculptures showcased inside, each chosen to help immerse every guest in this beautifully recreated bubble of Indochina. Cosy, quiet and dignified, the Lotus Room is ideal for families and couples, while the Rith Island is perfect for those who want to dine outdoors. This dining space is cool and inviting, and would especially appeal to those who want privacy. But, ultimately, it is the sight and aroma of the exquisitely prepared cuisine that really get the juices flowing in this restaurant.

With a choice of over 80 tantalising dishes on the à la carte evening menu, Basil Leaf does not, for a second, rest on its laurels. Each dish is as aesthetically

THIS PAGE (FROM TOP): The secluded Rith Island is ideal for private or corporate dining; Basil Leaf Restaurant offers a wide variety of Thai and Indochinese dishes.
OPPOSITE (CLOCKWISE FROM TOP): Every room is tastefully decorated; Basil Leaf can help organise a memorable event or function; enjoy a drink at the lounge.

pleasing and harmoniously balanced as if it were destined for the town's top food critic. Each item is crafted with the finest, freshest ingredients, flown in daily from the best food markets in Thailand, Vietnam, Laos and Cambodia.

Basil Leaf is renowned for the scope, invention and authenticity of its signature menu, created by chefs hand-picked from throughout Thailand for their wealth of expertise on local cuisine. Sample the Grilled Beef with Laotian Sauce, Thai Stir Fried Chicken with Long beans and Crispy Basil Leaves, or the Traditional Thai Clear Tom Yam. For Vietnamese fare, try the Grilled Salmon with Vietnamese Vermicelli in Lemongrass Sauce or the Vietnamese Spicy Prawns.

Delicious starters to look out for include the Cambodian Fish Salad with Aromatic Herbs, the Vietnamese Lotus Root Salad with Shredded Chicken and Prawns, and the delicate Saigonese Fresh Crystal Rolls prepared with a special chilli sauce and a

tangle of glass noodle salad. Fish aficionados will return time and again to retaste the melt-in-the-mouth succulence of the Thai baked salmon fillet, smothered in a dreamy red curry sauce, or to marvel at the mélange of steamed seafood served in a freshly hollowed out coconut. In addition to its exquisitely presented tasting plates, Basil Leaf boasts an impressive premium wine list, with examples from Australia's award-winning Yalumba winery, as well as from Tuscany, New Zealand, Chile and Argentina.

Basil Leaf is an excellent evening or event venue, with a cosy lounge, the Paradise and Lotus Rooms and an outdoor terrace. It can host 180 people comfortably. Whether for an intimate tête-à-tête or a company dinner or wedding reception, Basil Leaf Restaurant provides an unforgettable—and multi-sensory—culinary experience.

seats
180

food
Thai · Indochinese

drink
extensive wine list

features
authentic Thai and Indochinese cuisine · event planning

nearby
Crown Princess Hotel

contact
35 Jalan Damai, off Jalan Tun Razak 55000 Kuala Lumpur ·
telephone: +60.3.2166 1689 ·
facsimile: +60.3.2143 2689 ·
email: reservation@basilleafrestaurants.com ·
website: www.basilleafrestaurants.com

nerovivo

Though its on-street façade is sleek and elegant, Nerovivo is actually a humble, friendly trattoria in the very best Italian tradition. It is located in a refurbished colonial bungalow in the peaceful privacy of Ceylon Hill. Inside, a lively and passionately Italian atmosphere prevails.

Offering authentic homemade pasta, hearty main courses, delectable desserts and smoky, wood-fired pizza, Nerovivo is the brainchild of restaurateur Paolo Guiati. On top of the innovative menu and awe-inspiring wine list, he has created a pleasant atmosphere of genuine relaxation in which

guests are not afraid to raise their voices, laugh and chatter to their hearts' content, the Italian way.

Signature dishes at Nerovivo include the seafood soup and tiramisu. From the portions to the ingredients and unique presentation, they receive full marks here. The soup is a delicious mouthful of succulent frutti di mare in a tangy broth, while the tiramisu is heavenly. Piled within a delicate biscuit bowl, the crunchy surprises suspended in its light mousse give this timeless favourite a contemporary twist. The pannacotta with hot chocolate sauce melts in the mouth, too.

THIS PAGE: The stylish Nerovivo is a true find for lovers of authentic Italian food.

OPPOSITE (FROM TOP): Order a pre-dinner drink from the bar; al fresco dining is available.

...a humble, friendly trattoria in the very best Italian tradition.

seats
115

food
authentic Italian

drink
premium wines • Grappas • liqueurs

features
bar • al fresco dining • authentic wood fire pizza oven

nearby
Jalan Alor • Bukit Bintang • KL Tower

contact
3A, Jalan Ceylon, 50200 Kuala Lumpur •
telephone: +60.3.2070 3120 •
facsimile: +60.3.2070 3100 •
email: infor@nerovivo.com •
website: www.nerovivo.com

Recommended main courses include the Angus tenderloin with rich mushroom sauce, pan-fried lamb rack Milanese, grilled fresh jumbo prawns and roast cod fish in creola sauce. For pasta, try the linguine with scampi and the homemade potato gnocchi with fresh gorgonzola.

The pizza menu is extensive. Alongside staples such as tasty capricciosa, spicy diavola and rich gorgonzola pizza is the house special, the Nerovivo—juicy tomato, mozzarella, anchovies, sea scallops and rocket salad heaped onto crisp black olive dough. The ever-changing antipasto buffet displays such delights as beef carpaccio, seared imported scallops and pan-fried duck foie gras.

Nerovivo offers wine from Italy's most fêted producers, with many bottles imported directly from the winery. They are eminently affordable too, from light Pinot Grigio and bubbly Prosecco to bold, seductive Sicilians and grand Super Tuscans from the picturesque vineyards between Florence and Siena. The restaurant also boasts one of Malaysia's largest Grappa collections, as well as an impressive range of imported liqueurs and digestifs. The homemade frozen limoncello is designed to raise a few eyebrows.

With its warm hues broken up by striking exhibitions from locally based artists, Nerovivo is a welcoming trattoria to which one visit is rarely enough.

poppy collection

THIS PAGE: *Dance the night away at Passion.*

OPPOSITE (FROM LEFT): *Enjoy the sensual Thai menu at Poppy Garden; have a cosy lunch and intimate conversation at Bistro de Paris.*

Kuala Lumpur has become one of the most happening cities in Southeast Asia, boasting some of the world's tallest buildings, stylish shopping centres and sophisticated hotels. The streets are humming with activity and there is a buzz in the air; restaurants and cafés are sprouting up all over the place and a hot club scene has taken root. Central to this boom in entertainment and nightlife is the ultra-hip establishment Poppy Collection.

Housed in a modernist glass building with courtyards and al fresco terraces, award-winning Poppy Collection is located within walking distance of the Petronas Twin Towers in the Jalan P Ramlee district. It comprises two restaurants, bars and lounges,

each with its own personality. Evenings here are as exciting as nights spent bar-hopping in the city, but with none of the hassle.

Visitors to Poppy Collection might arrive for lunch at Bistro de Paris and take a scenic, street-side table to get a feel for life in downtown Kuala Lumpur with the Petronas Twin Towers as backdrop. The menu features fresh salad and barbecued dishes, with those irresistible Oriental flavours that come with Malay, Thai and Indonesian seasonings and condiments. The Poppy Garden Bar and Restaurant provides a cool, tranquil escape from the bustle of the city. Here, lush palm trees overhang the sleek, simple table settings, and subtle lighting sets the scene for a mellow tropical evening. At night, Poppy Collection transforms itself into a trendy hangout for Kuala Lumpur's hippest crowd. The dulcet tones of soul and jazz music fill the classy lounge bar Havanita, creating an atmosphere fit for the appreciation of premium wines, liqueurs and luxury cigars.

Passion is the place to be for some serious clubbing. The club boasts the chicest décor in town and lively music spun by local and international DJs. It is the temple of house music, having been the first club in Asia to host Café del Mar and other house meisters. Finally, Soul Seduction is the city's biggest outdoor RnB showcase, featuring international stars such as Jazzy Jeff. With everything that Poppy Collection has to offer, enthusiasts can keep coming back for more.

...evenings here are as exciting as nights spent bar-hopping in the city...

seats
Poppy Garden: 1,000 • Havanita: 100 •
Passion: 350 • Bistro de Paris: 100

food
Bistro De Paris: French •
Poppy Garden: sensual Thai

drink
fine spirits and concoctions

features
house music • live band • RnB music

nearby
Petronas Twin Towers • Rum Jungle •
clubs • bars

contact
8-1 Jalan P Ramlee, 50250 Kuala Lumpur •
telephone: +60.3.2141 8888 •
facsimile: +60.3.2148 1282 •
email: info@poppy-collection.com •
website: www.poppy-collection.com

souled out kuala lumpur

When entrepreneurs Fred Choo (also known as the 'Commander in Chief') and Michele Kwok (the 'First Lady') opened SOULed OUT Kuala Lumpur in September 1996, they could hardly have imagined the success it was to become. Ever since then, the café has grown from strength to strength, so that it now ranks as one of the city's foremost venues, whether for dining, drinking, dancing or simply hanging out and having a good time.

So, what are the secrets of the duo's success? First of all, a great eye for location. The original outlet was in the Mont Kiara Shoplex in the exclusive suburb of Bukit Kiara, but SOULed OUT's instant popularity prompted Fred and Michele to relocate the restaurant to an even more impressive address in Desa Sri Hartamas in 1999. Occupying a massive 557 sq m (6,000 sq ft) spread over two storeys—complete with a huge al fresco dining area fashioned into a pavement café—the new premises increased the seating capacity to a staggering 500 diners at any one time, so that no matter how big the party, there is always room for a few more.

THIS PAGE (FROM TOP): *SOULed OUT KL is casual and laid-back; from its humble beginnings as a neighbourhood café, the restaurant has become an iconic suburban destination.* OPPOSITE (FROM TOP): *The al fresco dining area at SOULed OUT; delicious Sake San pizza.*

seats
500

food
Western • North Indian • Malaysian

drinks
signature power and detox juices • extensive wine and cocktail list

features
theme parties • Booze Cruiser • nightly performances by SO Gaya dancers • complimentary valet parking

nearby
National Science Centre

contact
20 Jalan 30/70A, Desa Sri Hartamas 50480 Kuala Lumpur •
telephone: +60.3.2300 1955 •
facsimile: +60.3.2300 1989 •
email: yum_yum@souledout.com.my •
website: www.souledout.com.my

Secondly, the entrepreneurs harnessed one of Kuala Lumpur's greatest culinary assets—the wealth of national and international influences that the city benefits from. As a consequence, SOULed OUT offers an eclectic mix of over 100 different dishes showcasing Western, North Indian and Malaysian. This means that local favourites such as Fried Beef Noodles, Sang Har Mien and Chicken Makanwala happily sit side-by-side with more international staples such as wood-fired, thin-crust pizzas, cheese nachos and deep fried chicken wings.

Of course, it is not just the homestyle food that draws diners to SOULed OUT. The drinks list is extensive, with more than 100 cocktails, spirits, beers and wines to choose from, including such old favourites as the spectacular Flaming Lamborghinis and ever-delectable Strawberry Margaritas.

But perhaps the biggest reason for SOULed OUT's success is that it is a fun place to be. There is no attempt at pretension here, no unnecessary formality and nothing to compromise the wonderful dining and drinking experience that customers have come to expect. At SOULed OUT, the customer is most definitely king, as exemplified by the complimentary valet parking and the 'Booze Cruiser' service which ensures that patrons will be delivered home safely no matter how much they may have over-indulged. Add to all this a team of dedicated staff who are famous for putting their heart and soul into their work (hence, the café's name) and you have the perfect place to let your hair down and party. Indeed, SOULed OUT is all about fun and celebration, and it is a true-blue Malaysian restaurant with international flair that appeals to locals and tourists alike.

tamarind springs

The multi-award-winning Tamarind Springs restaurant is perched on the delicate line that divides Kuala Lumpur's actual and urban jungles. A leading proponent of the Jungle Luxe Dining philosophy, this chic, lounge-styled restaurant shines as the only property in Southeast Asia to be listed by the prestigious Relais & Chateaux group as a gourmet restaurant.

Surrounded by the luxuriant greens of Kuala Lumpur's forest reserve, Tamarind Springs is located within a spectacular tropical setting. Critically acclaimed by *Tatler* as 'Malaysia's Best Restaurant' for four consecutive years, Tamarind Springs has also garnered praise for its restaurant displays, winning the 'Most Creative Restaurant Display' award at the Malaysia International Gourmet Festival for 2004, 2006 and 2007.

The exotic fare at Tamarind Springs is as impressive as its interior design. Showcasing the authentic tastes, textures, scents and spices of Cambodia, Laos and Vietnam, guests get to sample a wide variety of Indochinese cuisine. House specialities to look out for include Vietnamese Pan Fried Salmon Parcels (with Asian pesto) and Laotian Sour Chicken and Coconut Soup. The Khmer-baked mussels

THIS PAGE (FROM TOP): Tamarind Springs offers Indochinese fare in a peaceful sanctuary; relax with a cocktail in the exotic atmosphere of the bar and lounge.

OPPOSITE (FROM TOP): One of the most popular Indochinese restaurants in the region, Tamarind Springs has won several accolades; the restaurant's Indochinese style is also evident in its décor.

seats
190

food
traditional Indochinese

drink
bar · lounge

features
spacious treetop verandahs · Zen Room · city shuttle service

nearby
Zoo Negara

contact
Jalan 1, Taman TAR, Ampang, 68000 Selangor ·
telephone: +60.3.4256 9300 ·
facsimile: +60.3.4251 9100 ·
email: info@tamarindrestaurants.com ·
website: www.tamarindrestaurants.com

in light curry sauce is also a must-try. Only the freshest ingredients are used to recreate the authentic Indochinese dishes at the restaurant. Be it a romantic, à la carte dinner for two, or a formal company event, Tamarind Springs will rise to the culinary occasion. With the Dine by Design service, guests can create their own personalised menus for private functions or weddings. To top it off, the restaurant's in-house Aspara Dancers will provide some exquisite entertainment.

Inside its teak interior, the restaurant is furnished with Asian sculptures, carvings and artefacts. Relaxed guests share their stories of the day, enjoying a unique dining experience in the sheltered, candlelit comfort of Tamarind's airy treetop balconies. The evening's ambient soundtrack blends in harmoniously, which can also be appreciated at the designer bar and lounge, where one can indulge in a pre- or post-dinner drink.

Ever since Tamarind Springs opened for business in 2002, it has attracted full houses and much press acclaim; it was recently voted 'Best Indochinese Restaurant' by *KL Lifestyle* magazine. Tamarind Springs is part of the Samadhi group's exclusive cache of intimate, boutique resorts, villas and restaurants. The fashionably rustic JapaMala Resorts on Tioman Island is a prime example of the pedigree of this niche group.

With international recognition and rave reviews, Tamarind Springs cannot fail to convert a new generation of diners to the flavours of Indochinese cuisine and to its own inimitable concept of Jungle Luxe Dining.

britishindia

THIS PAGE: Shop in the trendy tropical climate of BritishIndia.

OPPOSITE (FROM TOP): Apart from fashion wear, contemporary home products such as silk cushion covers can also be found in the stores; using mostly natural colours, clothes from BritishIndia are stylish in their simplicity.

When Pat Liew, a pioneer in the fashion retail industry, founded Malaysian fashion label BritishIndia in 1994, many were charmed by the colonial chic look of its apparel—mostly made from crisp linens, luxurious silk and cool cotton. They were in earthy tones and interpreted Indian wear with a modern twist, balancing embroidery with a sleeker look. With neutral and muted colours dominating the palette, BritishIndia's designs have captured the essence of the authentic style as seen from old, sepia-toned photographs belonging to the colonial era, where Liew first drew inspiration from.

However, Liew's love for this era was not shared by everyone. While she saw 19th-century colonial India as a time of great romance when larger-than-life characters set out on big adventures, others perceived it as a period of oppression and loss of independence. Yet, it is undeniable that the literature, architecture and culture of those days continue to inspire artists and writers today, and Liew is just one of them.

Driven by the nostalgic past, BritishIndia went on to win hearts around the world, namely in countries like Singapore, Brunei, Thailand, the Philippines, Australia and the

products
clothes • furniture

features
colonial chic style wear and décor

nearby
Petronas Twin Towers

contact
G305A, 1 Utama Shopping Centre
Lebuh Bandar Utama, 47800 Petaling Jaya •
telephone: +60.3.7724 1822

Ground Floor, Great Eastern Mall
No. 303 Jalan Ampang, 50450 Kuala Lumpur •
telephone: +60.3.4253 5266

Lot 111A and B, 1st floor, Suria KLCC, Kuala
Lumpur City Centre, 50088 Kuala Lumpur •
telephone: +60.3.2166 2282

email: customerservice@bi.com.my

United Arab Emirates because of its cultural approach to fashion. Its boutiques stand shoulder to shoulder with luxury brand names such as Gucci and Ralph Lauren in gleaming, upmarket malls around the region.

BritishIndia's East meets West concept appeals to both fashionistas and well-travelled individuals, who can get hold of a little piece of exotica by simply stopping by its stores. The BritishIndia line evokes a Bohemian feel—its exotic touch is retained, yet designs are more than stylish and modern enough for the fashion capitals of Paris and London.

Holistic considerations are very much part of the company's working ethos, as seen from the introduction of its Yoga Collection in 2002. Using stretchable material and calming colours such as white and light turquoise, clothes from this collection combine comfort and style for the ideal yoga session.

BritishIndia's colonial chic extends to its stores. The walls of the boutiques are often of a creamy shade, providing a clean canvas to showcase their elegantly carved furniture. The soothing colours of the interiors are well complemented by the giant pots of palm leaves or tropical plants that are part of the décor. Entering a BritishIndia store is akin to taking a step back into the colonial past, when the pace of life was more relaxed and architecture had a romantic feel to it.

When customers, enchanted by the furnishings, began asking to buy the lamps and richly carved furniture at the store, it only seemed natural for BritishIndia to diversify and expand its offerings to include items for the home such as bedlinen, furniture, silk cushion covers and even garden pots. Indeed, the colonial era may be a thing of the past, but one may still own a piece of it through BritishIndia and bring it home.

ombak asia

Enticing visitors inside with its friendly ethos and the gentle lilt of exotic world music, the Ombak store is every interior design lover's dream. A feast for the eyes, it is laden with unique handcrafted artefacts from regions across Southeast Asia. Entering the store provides an experience akin to exploring an art gallery, design studio or the home of your most aesthetically astute friend, with the added bonus that everything within may be bought and conveniently shipped home, not merely complimented and coveted.

Over 90 per cent of the products in Ombak are authentically handmade by indigenous craftspeople. As a result, each piece overflows with character and individuality, as will the rooms within which each piece will eventually find a home. From artisan crafted cushions and unique hand-carved armchairs, to gleaming hardwood bowls, Buddhist busts and racks of Iban spears, Ombak is full of eye-catching furniture, hangings and objets d'art, patiently waiting to take someone's breath away as the ultimate home decoration or wonderful wedding gift.

Run by designer Simon Gan, Ombak is not merely a retail outfit. It is also responsible for the sophisticated artworks of several world-class hotels throughout the East. To cherry pick a few esteemed properties, Simon and his team have acted as art consultants to the Mandarin Oriental Tokyo, Mandarin Oriental Singapore and the Four Seasons Resort Langkawi, and this luxury hotel list grows longer day by day. To make any home as impressive as these top-ranking hotels, simply spend a few imaginative hours and immerse yourself within the stone, glass, silk and woodcraft of Ombak.

Simon follows his heart rather than his mind in deciding what to stock in this aesthete's paradise. His guiding impulse is a desire to fuse Eastern inspiration with Western sensibilities, creating a world in which ancient tradition sits comfortably alongside more contemporary themes. Simon's tastes are not faddish, and he shies away from attempts to pin down the transient and ever-shifting goals of fashion. Instead, his high quality displays—from striking yet complementary to harmoniously understated—simply showcase the artists and ideas that have moved him and are classic and timeless in their appeal.

The space and mood within Ombak can be likened to those of a home. At times it evokes a bazaar with a multi-coloured riot of patterns, textures and fabrics. Yet turn around and there lies an elegantly lit showcase of individual statues, figurines and sculptures, each chosen with as much flair and consideration as if it were already gracing Simon's own impeccably furnished home.

To explore these beautiful peaks of Southeast Asian craftsmanship, art and design step in to the beguiling world of Ombak. Never before has the fusion of worlds old and new been so stylish.

Never before has the fusion of worlds old and new been so stylish.

products
authentically handmade furniture • artefacts •
antiques • objets d'art

features
art consultancy

nearby
Petronas Art Gallery

contact
Lot No. 301-A, 3rd floor, Suria KLCC, Kuala
Lumpur City Centre, 50088 Kuala Lumpur •
telephone: +60.3.2161 9600 •
facsimile: +60.3.2161 9613 •
email: ombakklcc@hotmail.com •
website: www.ombak.com.my

purser's choice

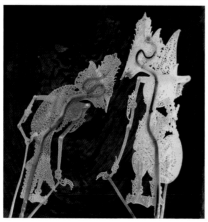

In Malaysia's thriving capital, increasing homogenisation is slowly but surely making its mark on the high street. This makes havens of originality such as Purser's Choice jump out from the sea of mass market brands, as refreshing as an iced green tea on a hot and humid afternoon.

Purveyors of fine furniture and beautifully restored artefacts, decorative items and gift ideas, Purser's Choice is a quintessential stop-off point for discerning travellers and expatriates seeking authentic, island crafted rarities, or colonial-styled as well as modern furniture featuring old, recycled and grade A new teak.

Visionary pioneers in decorating the lives and homes of Kuala Lumpur's style-savvy cognoscenti since 1993, this melting pot of contemporary Asian inspiration boasts a plethora of unique products and unusual collectibles. The product line is divided into two categories that complement each other well: exquisitely made teak furniture and delightful home decorative pieces. Highlights include terracotta pot lamps, tribal fabrics, spun-bamboo and wrought-iron artefacts. The emphasis throughout is on traditional Javanese and Balinese designs.

There are intricately painted and traditionally carved panels from Madura, an island off the northeast coast of Java with its own distinctive cultural and linguistic heritage. There are colourful, handwoven ikats, sarong-styled fabrics woven into a wealth of designs to represent wealth, prestige and even magical powers. Being lightweight and unbreakable, ikats make the perfect travel gift or souvenir.

For use as an unusual side table or simply to add an exotic focal point to any room, opt for a grobok, a traditionally carved teak trunk. And for those with grander designs in mind, there is an impressive array of finely crafted teak furniture from genuine Indonesian craftsmen. All furniture and complementary pieces are sourced from Indonesia. Purser's Choice also boasts a range of designer furniture in contemporary designs that reflect and provide a serene resort and tropical feel.

Located in Kuala Lumpur's Bangsar Village II, Purser's Choice provides a calm escape from the rowdy market melee. From its expertly restored antique pieces to modern innovations and decorations from Java, Bali and beyond, Purser's Choice boasts an excellent reputation for friendly customer service and authentic craftsmanship of the highest quality. The helpful staff at the shop will be pleased to organise the shipping of any gifts or purchases to destinations around the globe. Wholesale purchases can also be arranged.

Whether for aesthetic pleasure, as a special occasion gift or for practical everyday usage, the carefully selected products of Purser's Choice will surpass every expectation, acting as lingering mementoes of an unforgettable holiday. The store is small

...a name synonymous with fine quality, taste and style.

enough to extend a helpful personalised service to its visitors, yet large enough to fulfil the most diverse requests. Purser's Choice is a name synonymous with fine quality, taste and style. For attractive, stylish furnishings and accent pieces that add a contemporary Asian twist to any home or office, or one of a kind bric-a-brac and gift items, there is no better place to go than the gem of a store that is Purser's Choice.

products
teak furniture • home accessories • lamps

features
traditional Javanese and Balinese designs

nearby
Mid Valley City • Bangsar Shopping Centre • Bangsar LRT station • KL Sentral • One Bangsar restaurants

contact
Bangsar Village II, 2nd floor, Units 1b and 2
2 Jalan Telawi 1, 59100 Kuala Lumpur •
telephone: +60.3.2282 1928 •
facsimile: +60.3.2282 1923 •
email: info@purserschoice.com •
website: www.purserschoice.com

royal selangor

There are certain brand names that truly resonate; they are associated with fine craftsmanship, innovation, design and durability. In the particular case of pewter, it is Royal Selangor. Unknown to many, this prestigious name in tableware and decorative pieces has its home in Setapak Jaya, Kuala Lumpur, where pewter products are made in the largest factory of its kind in the world.

Exported to over 20 countries and sold in distinguished department stores the world over, Royal Selangor has won several international design awards and a mere glimpse at the company's catalogue makes it easy to see why.

Traditional tankards, intricate picture frames and exquisite vases are but a few examples of the myriad of highly desirable home accessories available. Fashionistas will also be pleased that they can browse through Royal Selangor's vast collection of stylish jewellery and unique accessories.

And fortunately someone at Royal Selangor had the inspired idea of opening a stunning visitor centre to celebrate the art of creating fine pewter, and share the company's fascinating history since its establishment in 1885.

Like all things created by Royal Selangor, the Visitor Centre is a masterpiece and a must-see for those passing through Kuala Lumpur. Built in 2004 and located at the site of the factory and company headquarters, this is something that will appeal to the whole family. Visitors first pass through The Gallery, which comprises interactive and educational exhibits that focus on the company's origins and the qualities and attributes of the alloy. A remarkable replica of the Petronas Twin Towers made out of 7,062 pewter tankards is sure to impress, as will the musical Chamber of Chimes and giant weighing scale.

THIS PAGE (FROM TOP): Add style to any table with these Zuii salt and pepper shakers; this Nick Munro tea set makes afternoon tea an even more special ritual.

OPPOSITE (FROM TOP): 1885, the year the company was founded. Sheathed in pewter, this exhibit is part of the Royal Selangor Visitor Centre; learn about pewter's rich past, its exciting present and beautiful future at the Visitor Centre.

products
pewter homeware and gifts

features
Visitor Centre for educational tours • School of
Hard Knocks pewtersmithing workshop

nearby
Kuala Lumpur City Centre • Petronas Twin Towers

contact
4 Jalan Usahawan 6, Setapak Jaya
53300 Kuala Lumpur •
telephone: +60.3.4145 6122 •
facsimile: +60.3.4022 3000 •
email: visitorcentre@royalselangor.com.my •
website: www.visitorcentre.royalselangor.com

Given its total mastery in the realm of pewter—much of it still done by hand—Royal Selangor's craftsmen have stretched the limits of its versatility, achieving an astonishing array of textures and finishes that can be witnessed in the Hall of Finishes.

With some 100 exhibits on display, the museum showcases many interesting elements, offering a peek into Royal Selangor's rich and intriguing past through various exhibits of pewter, some of which date back to the late 1800s.

The Factory Tour takes visitors to the very heart of Royal Selangor's manufacturing process where they can watch how pewter is made from start to finish—from casting, filing and polishing to hammering and engraving. At the School of Hard Knocks, visitors can participate in a pewtersmithing workshop and create their very own dish—a favourite among the young and old alike.

The pièce de résistance, however, is the spacious, 1,672-sq-m (18,000-sq-ft) retail store, where visitors can choose from the world's largest selection of Royal Selangor merchandise, including fine jewellery from Selberan and sterling silver from Comyns, sister companies of Royal Selangor.

While the Royal Selangor Visitor Centre may not be the most obvious option for sightseers in Kuala Lumpur, it is by far one of the most worthwhile.

the carat club, kuala lumpur

Cut, colour, clarity and carat weight—the 'four Cs' that are all anyone needs to know when buying a diamond. Though seemingly simple and straightforward in theory, purchasing a diamond is more complex in practice, as befits a gemstone that is coveted and admired the world over. And this is where Kuala Lumpur's exclusive The Carat Club steps in.

The Carat Club is not just any jeweller, for diamonds are not just any jewel. This fact is intuitively understood and passionately communicated at this high-class diamond and rare gem boutique. The ambience is elegant and unhurried, so intimate and inclusive that the boutique exudes the aura of a members' only club.

The Carat Club is located within a contemporary bungalow in Kuala Lumpur's stylish Bangsar district. This modern-day treasure trove offers a fine display of life's indulgent luxuries, with gleaming rubies and eye-catching emeralds displayed alongside a myriad of exquisitely cut diamonds, each and every one exuding a mesmerising fire. With informative screenings and tantalising confectionery and coffee on the house, The Carat Club escalates the retail experience to an entirely new level.

The driving force behind the jeweller's unique concept is Chan Boon Yong, a second-generation diamond specialist whose 'with knowledge comes passion' philosophy

THIS PAGE (FROM TOP): Exquisite diamond ring and earrings; The Carat Club's boutique is sleek, classy and stylish.
OPPOSITE (FROM TOP): Draw envious stares with these La Nouvelle Bague bangles and Calgaro choker; Lunari rings designed by Stefan Hafner.

products
diamonds • gems • jewellery

features
custom jewellery design • designer jewellery brands • personalised appointments • cleaning and preservation services

nearby
Bangsar Shopping Complex • Bangsar Village Shopping Centre

contact
Boutique
119 Jalan Maarof, Taman Bangsar
59000 Kuala Lumpur •
telephone: +60.3.2284 8618 •
facsimile: +60.3.2284 8663 •
email: bsr@thecaratclub.com

Head Office
99L Jalan Tandok, off Jalan Maarof
59000 Kuala Lumpur •
telephone: +60.3.2284 8620 •
facsimile: +60.3.2284 8662 •
website: www.thecaratclub.com

courses through every element of The Carat Club. This English-educated and award-winning entrepreneur narrowed his focus from wholesaling polished diamonds to concentrating on the premium end of an already prestigious market. As a result, The Carat Club opened its gleaming doors in 1997.

Today, The Carat Club's unsurpassed portfolio has widened from enticingly affordable solitaires, bracelets and earrings to include European designer jewellery brands, many seen for the first time in Asia. Names worth seeking out include Italy's innovative Adelio Rossini, the fashionista favourite Calgaro, the stunning creations of La Nouvelle Bague, Gavello's ultra-modern pieces and Stefan Hafner's dramatically glamorous collections.

Boon Yong's personal brainchild, The Love Diamond, is the signature product of The Carat Club. This ideal cut diamond, Malaysia's first internationally renowned diamond brand, features eight hearts and eight arrows in perfect symmetry and excellent polish. Shining with brilliance, The Love Diamond is a definite must-see for romantic suitors and fiancés.

Aside from its excellent portfolio, what sets The Carat Club apart is the time devoted by its welcoming team of professionals to ensure that clients develop the necessary knowledge to appreciate the worth of their purchases. This warm service, coupled with high-quality products, makes for a match made in jewellery heaven.

The Carat Club knows that diamonds are such a significant investment. Every purchase, therefore, comes with a certificate of value and authenticity, as well as after-care cleaning and preservation services to ensure a glittering future for each exquisite piece—and peace of mind for the buyer. Celebrate the start of a lifelong relationship with one of Asia's most passionate jewellers, with a beautiful and sparkling gem from Kuala Lumpur's fêted The Carat Club.

westmalaysia

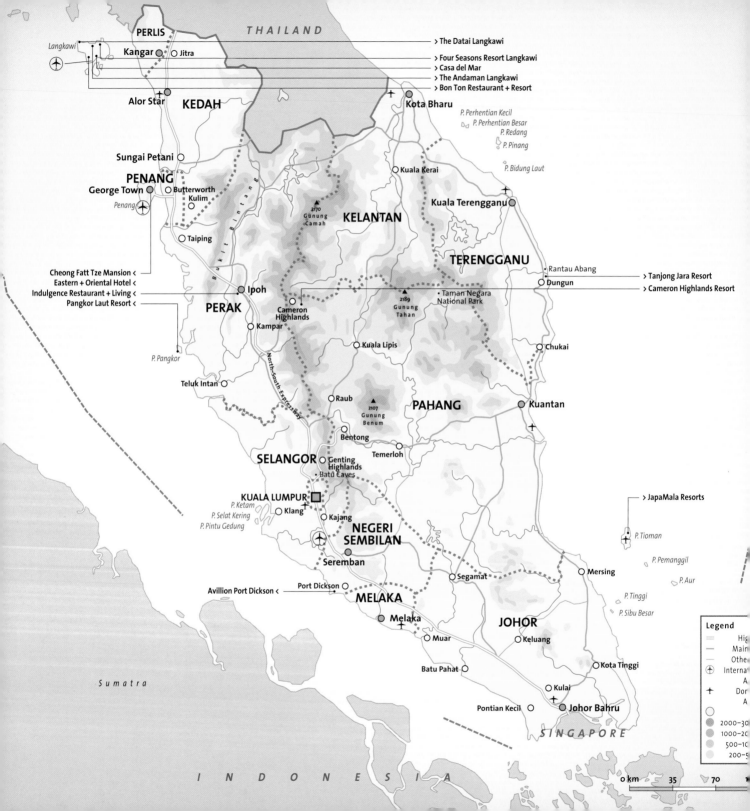

THAILAND

PERLIS
Kangar ◯ Jitra
Langkawi
✈

> The Datai Langkawi
> Four Seasons Resort Langkawi
> Casa del Mar
> The Andaman Langkawi
> Bon Ton Restaurant + Resort

Alor Star
KEDAH
Kota Bharu
P. Perhentian Kecil
P. Perhentian Besar
P. Redang
P. Pinang

Sungai Petani
P. Bidung Laut

PENANG
George Town ◯ Butterworth
Kulim
Penang ✈

Kuala Kerai

2170
Gunung
Camah

KELANTAN

Kuala Terengganu

Taiping

Bukit Bintang

Cheong Fatt Tze Mansion ‹
Eastern + Oriental Hotel ‹
Indulgence Restaurant + Living ‹
Pangkor Laut Resort ‹

TERENGGANU

Rantau Abang
> Tanjong Jara Resort
Dungun
> Cameron Highlands Resort

Ipoh

PERAK
Cameron
Highlands

2189
Gunung
Tahan

• Taman Negara
National Park

Kampar

North-South Expressway

P. Pangkor

Kuala Lipis

Chukai

Teluk Intan

Raub
2107
Gunung
Benum

PAHANG

Kuantan

Bentong

SELANGOR
Genting
Highlands
• Batu Caves

Temerloh

KUALA LUMPUR ☐
P. Ketam
P. Selat Kering
P. Pintu Gedung

Klang
Kajang

> JapaMala Resorts

P. Tioman

NEGERI
SEMBILAN

P. Pemanggil

Seremban

Segamat

Mersing

P. Aur

Avillion Port Dickson ‹
Port Dickson

P. Tinggi

MELAKA

P. Sibu Besar

Melaka

JOHOR

Muar
Keluang

Batu Pahat

Kota Tinggi

Kulai

Pontian Kecil

Johor Bahru

Sumatra

SINGAPORE

I N D O N E S I A

0 km   35   70

west malaysia

where the monsoon winds meet

Each of the 11 states that make up West Malaysia has its own identity. Despite this abundant variety, they have more in common with one another than with East Malaysia, which has quite a different racial mix. The ethnic cocktail of West Malaysia is mainly determined by the relative proportions of Malays, Chinese and Indians who live there.

The East Coast of the peninsula has a Malay majority, while the West Coast has a high proportion of Chinese and Indian descent. From the visitor's point of view this generally means a contrast between the rural idylls and unspoilt beaches of the East Coast, and the ceaseless economic expansion of the West Coast. Both halves of the peninsula have seen considerable migration from countryside to cities. The East Coast has the growing metropolises of Kuantan, Kuala Terengganu and Kota Bharu. On the West, the old commercial centres—Kuala Lumpur, Ipoh and George Town—are growing too. The last of these is unusual for having a colonial name in a country which has phased out most traces of its pre-independence past. Street names have been changed and entire towns have been renamed, including the former Port Swettenham which is now Port Klang.

West Malaysia has more than just an East and a West Coast. There is also a North and a South Coast, although the different states within these subdivisions don't always have a great deal in common. The most southerly state, Johor, is definitely part of the West Coast in terms of development. The far northern states of Perlis and Kedah have more in common with the East Coast states of Kelantan and Terengganu. Running from the north to the south of this narrow peninsula is a central sliver of land—mostly mountainous and sparsely inhabited. The climate is similar throughout, although some areas are more prone to heavy rainfall than others. Flooding on the East Coast is an annual event. Elsewhere it comes as an uncomfortable but fairly regular surprise, hence traditional houses built on stilts are a common sight.

There are resorts of international standard all over the peninsula. Most of these are located by the sea, although there are many inland locations that have taken advantage of the growing interest in eco-tourism. Taman Negara is the largest eco-destination in the country, offering more than 4,000 sq km (988,422 acres) of ancient rainforest. There is an unrivalled variety of wildlife, although sightings of tigers and rhinoceros have been sparse in recent years. Monkeys are always visible in the forest, just as they are in Malaysia's 'concrete jungles'. Wildlife preservation has become a high priority for Malaysians as well as concerned foreigners. Organisations such as the Malaysian Nature Society attract an upmarket membership.

THIS PAGE: *The east coast of West Malaysia is a haven for marine life. Turtles and other endangered species are the main attraction for divers.*

PAGE 122: *Beaches such as Tanjung Rhu on Langkawi island have some of the most spectacular sunsets to be seen in Malaysia.*

urban renewal

At the other end of the touristic spectrum are West Malaysia's cities. These are places in which to admire the energy that pulses through one of Southeast Asia's most vigorous 'tiger economies'. The older towns still have a colonial heart that is equipped with historic buildings and tree-lined streets. Heritage conservation is usually a rather delayed afterthought. George Town in Penang has tried harder than most, and the rewards are some spectacularly restored temples, mansions and clan association buildings. The most popular are the Khoo Kongsi and the Cheong Fatt Tze Mansion, although the entire neighbourhood has enough history for the movie *Anna and the King* to be filmed there, with Jodie Foster and Chow Yun Fatt as the lead stars.

Most of the peninsula's older monuments are from the late 19th to the early 20th century, a time when huge numbers of migrants left China for the unexploited potential of the 'Southern Sea'. Much of the late Qing-dynasty culture they brought with them is visible only in Malaysia, Singapore and Indonesia. West Malaysia has the nation's oldest buildings, mostly from the Portuguese and Dutch periods. Melaka has what is left of a Portuguese fort, A Famosa, from the 16th century, saved from destruction by Sir Stamford Raffles. Going back further, the northern state of Kedah has the ruins of a Hindu-Buddhist temple complex from at least 1,000 years ago.

West Malaysia's urban development is the result of 19th-century Chinese immigration. The rural environment was maintained by the British colonial authorities as a sanctuary for the Malay population. Indian workers were imported to service rubber plantations, although this community also made a prominent contribution to the growth of towns.

These days, the old colonial divisions of labour have merged into a less-structured society. The activities that made the peninsula so profitable in the past have changed. Tin and rubber industries have given way to manufacturing and financial services. West

THIS PAGE: The waterfront at George Town has been smartened up considerably in recent years.

OPPOSITE (FROM LEFT): Kek Lok Si Temple is one of Penang's most famous landmarks. In addition to its tourism value, the temple is used extensively by the local Chinese community during festivals; Cheong Fatt Sze Mansion was restored and repainted in its original indigo blue.

Malaysia has used its position as a stable, prosperous Muslim-majority nation to develop Islamic banking and insurance. The country is now the world's largest issuer of Islamic debt.

Tourism has also been given a big push. The benefits of this are felt by residents as well as tourists. There are more activities than ever before. These include 'health tourism', which brings bargain-hunting tourists to well-equipped, professionally staffed hospitals in West Malaysia for everything from cosmetic procedures to major surgery.

Whether it is art galleries or wave pools, West Malaysia has been transformed in the decades following Independence. In 1957 there were no hotels of international quality; the Federal Hotel had to be built to accommodate the dignitaries who came to Kuala Lumpur for the Independence ceremonies. Nowadays there is a massive surplus of hotel accommodation. Going another step forward, there are now boutique hotels. The most recent of these is in Ipoh: Indulgence Hotel combines colonial grandeur with modern comfort and convenience, and boasts an excellent restaurant.

West Malaysia has been an entrepôt between the Orient and the Occident ever since merchant ships discovered the Strait of Malacca, making it among the busiest shipping lanes in the world. On average, more than 50,000 vessels pass through this narrow stretch of water every year.

Malaysia has also been trying to compete with Singapore for shipping business, which handles more containers than anywhere else. Port of Tanjung Pelepas and the new Iskandar Development Region in Johor are trying to change the regional trade dynamics. This dynamism is very much a part of modern Malaysia, which is shaking off its image as Singapore's sleepy northern neighbour.

Malaysia is also a land with a long history of providing a multi-lingual welcome to visitors from all over the world. The appeal works well enough for the country, to have developed a significant position as a retirement home for overseas citizens on the lookout for friendly faces and endless sunshine.

...an entrepôt between the Orient and the Occident ever since...

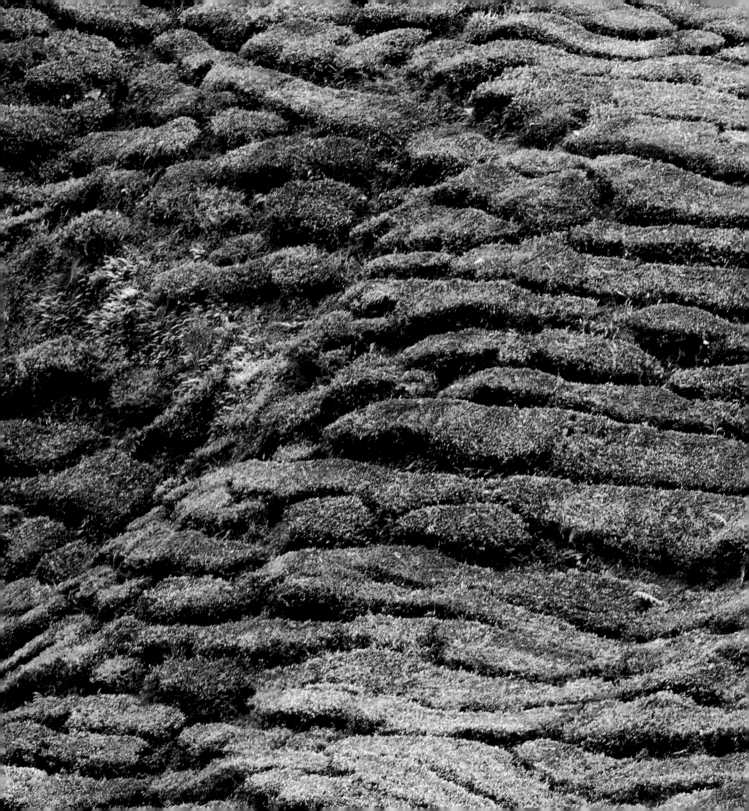

avillion port dickson

Port Dickson boasts an 18-km (11-mile) curve of white-sand coastline, and is a relatively undiscovered hideaway just over an hour south of Kuala Lumpur. Nestled among lush foliage, the uniquely designed Avillion Port Dickson, a beach resort and spa, is one of the highlights, emulating the essence of a traditional Malay fishing village with liberal lashings of five-star luxury for good measure. Avillion is a versatile chameleon of a resort. A premier business and leisure destination, it over-delivers whether for a

fun family vacation, as backdrop to the ultimate sunset beach wedding and honeymoon experience, or as a venue for a candlelit beach dinner under the stars. Fondly called 'the love resort' by *Singapore Brides*, Avillion has also received glowing praise from *Her World Brides* and *Travel Malaysia* with inclusive pre-wedding packages for the glowing bride-to-be.

Children will return exhausted after frolicking in the family-friendly Village Pool. For adult adrenaline-seekers, the water sports

THIS PAGE (CLOCKWISE FROM TOP): *Feel the sea breeze and enjoy the sunset from the balcony; take a dip in the quaint surroundings of Avillion; the Avillion four-poster bed is one of many modern comforts to be found at the resort.*

OPPOSITE (FROM TOP): *The sandy beaches are ideal for private outdoor functions; look forward to a peaceful retreat at Avillion Port Dickson.*

...an eclectic mix of classic and contemporary Malay cuisine.

centre offers fishing, boating and kayak hire, the ideal cruising speed at which to explore the endless intricacies of the local coastline. Couples will prefer the serenity of the adults-only Cochin pool, resplendent in a lush, jungle-fringed setting, open 24 hours for those spontaneous nocturnal dips.

Clustered near Avillion's private beaches lapped by waters of turquoise and cobalt are its distinguishing feature—the luxuriously appointed Water Chalets. Stretching out from tropical shores, their interiors combine old world charm with every modern convenience. Spread across seven wings to ensure privacy, their sun-warmed decks float between the glistening sea and the infinite skies with transparent linen draped across the four-poster beds for that extra touch of romance.

Those with an appetite for adventure may have heard of intrepid English explorer Lord Jennings Avery, credited with the discovery of Port Dickson. His cultural heritage has been artfully preserved at Avillion, with suites named after the characters in his riveting diaries. Each Garden Chalet, Water Chalet and Avery Suite provides sea and sunset views, to be enjoyed from the inviting pangkin, or daybed. Avillion staff can organise in-room reflexology or traditional Malay full-body massage if the gym or tennis court options seem a little too strenuous.

Avillion offers an eclectic mix of classic and contemporary Malay cuisine. The Village Court poolside restaurant offers a winning

mixture of Western and local dishes, its fresh seafood barbecues being the culinary highlight. With a phenomenal view over sea and shore, The Crow's Nest Restaurant is the ideal choice for a little candlelit intimacy. From open-air performances at the gallery to the safari-themed karaoke lounge, evenings always sparkle at this tropical hotspot.

For the ultimate indulgence, guests can head to the recently-opened Avi Spa. Relaxing treatments and programmes aside, the spa also offers breathtaking views of the sea.

Escape the frantic pace of city life, and exchange the crowds of Kuala Lumpur, for Avillion's relaxed getaway.

rooms
259

food
Crow's Nest: local and international ·
Village Court: seafood

drink
Jungle Fringe Karaoke & Bar · The Galley Lounge

features
open-air showers · air-conditioning ·
tennis court · gym · steam and sauna room ·
kids' cabin and playroom · pet farm ·
spice farm · in-house wedding planners ·
event specialists

business
conference, banqueting and ballroom facilities ·
business centre · function rooms

nearby
Cape Rachado Lighthouse · Seremban ·
Kuala Lumpur

contact
3rd Mile, Jalan Pantai, 71000 Port Dickson
Negeri Sembilan ·
telephone: +60.6.647 6688 ·
facsimile: +60.6.647 7688 ·
email: res@avillion.com.my ·
website: www.avillion.com

bon ton restaurant + resort

It all began in 1987 with a restaurant in an old colonial bungalow in Kuala Lumpur. Bon Ton Restaurant was a quaint place to eat; it had an antiques gallery and a wine room and was the toast of the fine dining scene. Given its popularity, it was not long before Bon Ton expanded to Langkawi. Offering seafood, 'Western with spice' cuisine and Nyonya food, the restaurant started operations in the island in 1994, in an undeveloped coconut plantation bordered by wetlands and a lagoon filled with lotus flowers.

From 1995 to 2004, under the watchful eye of owner Narelle McMurtrie, eight antique Malay kampung houses and a Chinese provisions shop were relocated to the plantation. These elegant buildings, ranging from 50 to 120 years old, were carefully dismantled then painstakingly reassembled. Local carpenters, skilled in making old kampung houses, restored these houses which were once left to rot. Thus, Bon Ton Restaurant and Resort was born.

The kampung houses are now fitted with modern trappings such as bathroom facilities, ceiling fans, TV, DVD and CD players, and airconditioning. They are now elegant villas, a place where holidaymakers can have a taste of Malay village life, yet enjoy the comfort of modern amenities.

Take the 120-year-old Palm Villa. One can gaze at the pool from the big windows, which have beautiful, carved panels on top. The Silk Villa has plantation-style shutters that open out to tropical gardens. This house is perfect for families; it has two queen beds in one room and two single beds in another.

The other villas—Blue Ginger, Yellow Orchid, Black Coral, White Frangipani, Laguna and Cahaya—come with their own ethnic touches such as intricate Malay carvings on

...nurturing culture, creativity and nature seems to be the resort's motto.

rooms
8 villas

food
Nam Restaurant: Western and Nyonya

drink
Chin Chin Lounge Bar • Pool Bar & Sunset Deck • wine cellar

features
high-speed Internet access • lap pool • jacuzzi • massage room

nearby
Kuah • Telaga Harbour • Datai Bay • Ibrahim Hussein Museum • Gunung Raya

contact
Pantai Cenang, 07000 Langkawi, Kedah • telephone: +60.4.955 3643 • facsimile: +60.4.955 4791 • email: info@bontonresort.com.my • website: www.bontonresort.com.my

wooden walls. At night, spotlights illuminate the houses, casting an ethereal glow over these once humble homes. These villas have furniture made from rich tropical wood, and white, gauzy drapes hanging from high, four-poster beds give the accommodation a grand and romantic feel.

The former Chinese provisions shop is now Chin Chin, an Asian bar and lounge. The refurbished shop house evokes nostalgia, with the original store plaque still hanging on its walls and marble-topped tables outside reminiscent of those in kopitiams.

At Bon Ton Resort, guests are treated like family. Those so inclined can cook in the resort's kitchen after buying their ingredients from Langkawi's markets, or mix their own cocktails behind the bar. Guests who do not want to get their hands dirty can sample the exceptional food at Nam Restaurant. However, Bon Ton Resort is not merely a place to soak up the sun's rays and satisfy cravings for good food. Guests can also feast their eyes on works of art, thanks to Narelle's 'artist in residence programme' that allows local artists to exhibit their works in the resort. The owner's passion for all things Langkawi has even extended to creating a sanctuary for the island's stray dogs and cats.

Narelle's personal touches are clearly evident around Bon Ton Restaurant and Resort. Nurturing culture, creativity and nature seems to be the resort's motto and this will certainly please holidaymakers who want a luxurious and out-of-the-box experience in a friendly and relaxed setting.

cameron highlands resort

Cameron Highlands, located in the state of Pahang and around 200 km (124 miles) north of Kuala Lumpur, is Malaysia's little English village in the hills. It is the only place in Malaysia where tea plantations, strawberry farms and quaint Tudor-styled cottages can be found together. During the days of colonial rule, the Highlands was the favourite getaway spot for the British because it gave them a taste of home. With a daily average temperature of 20°C (68°F), its cool climate also provides a welcome respite from Malaysia's tropical heat.

Perched on a hillock with a view of a golf course and lush green hills, the stately Cameron Highlands Resort is a luxurious retreat located right in the middle of the Highlands' famous tea plantations.

The 56-room boutique resort exudes nostalgic colonial charm; guests are welcomed by the sight of tall French doors decorated with white curtains and plantation shutters that open to gorgeous views of the green, undulating hills and let in the crisp, fresh air. The king-sized four-poster bed is the highlight of the rooms, while timber flooring, timber-beamed ceilings and rich, dark wood furniture upholstered with cream-coloured fabrics give the resort the feel of a charming English manor. There is even an open fireplace in the resort's Reading Room, the perfect place to curl up in a leather couch with a book while savouring a cup of tea from the resort's extensive tea menu.

And since Cameron Highlands is renowned for its tea plantations—among them the famous Boh Tea Plantation—it is not surprising that tea, once a prized commodity in colonial Malaya, plays a huge part in the resort experience. Guests may have a traditional English afternoon tea with

rooms
56

food
Gonbei: Japanese • The Dining Room: Western •
Jim Thompson Tea Room: afternoon tea

drink
Highlands Bar

features
gym • Spa Village • tea bath • outdoor cabanas •
Jim Thompson boutique • Reading Room •
snooker • grand ballroom • function rooms

nearby
Semai villages • tea plantations • cactus valley•
strawberry farms • butterfly garden • rose
centre • Sam Poh temple • Mount Brinchang •
18-hole golf course

contact
39000 Tanah Rata, Cameron Highlands, Pahang •
telephone: +60.5.491 1100 •
facsimile: +60.5.491 1800 •
email: travelcentre@ytlhotels.com.my •
website: www.cameronhighlandsresort.com

finger sandwiches or Cameron Highlands strawberries in the elegant Jim Thompson Tea Room, a room dedicated to the late American architect, textile merchant and former CIA agent who went missing during an afternoon walk in Cameron Highlands on Easter Sunday in 1967. And if guests feel inclined for a spot of literature, the Reading Room has a variety of books available. Tea evidently enjoys a special role within the resort, for even the resort's award-winning Spa Village has a signature tea bath ritual.

Still, Cameron Highlands Resort doesn't forget its Asian identity. The resort's gardens are carefully cultivated to reflect a fusion of East and West. Huge, earthy clay pots house lush tropical palms and Balinese-inspired fountains line the corridor of the Spa Village. Fine Thai silk can be found at the Jim Thompson Boutique and the Spa Village offers local exotic treatments such as the ancient Tunku Batu treatment and a 50-minute Malay massage in either the indoor or outdoor treatment rooms, where guests can have their tired bodies rubbed down with the warm Minyak Lumur Sakti ointment.

The Cameron Highlands Resort is warm, inviting and exudes an elegant air—a European world in a tropical land, the ideal remedy for the weary traveller tired from the travails of urban living.

casa del mar

It is like a little piece of Spain in the middle of a tropical island—Casa del Mar, which means 'home by the sea' in Spanish, is located on Langkawi Island's Pantai Cenang Beach, and its name reflects the kind of experience guests will get. With only 34 rooms, one can look forward to a peaceful retreat at this boutique resort.

Magnificent palms fan out at the entrance of Casa del Mar, and the people who designed this Spanish-villa-like resort prefer a more intimate approach. Instead of an extravagant lobby, the first sight that greets weary travellers is a spacious and cosy living room, complete with sofas furnished with plump, flower print cushions and a bookcase full of books. A home by the sea indeed, for the folks at Casa del Mar truly take their name very seriously.

The Mediterranean theme is carried into the guestrooms. In the Deluxe Rooms, fans spin lazily from the ceiling—there's air-conditioning, of course—beds are plush and floor-to-ceiling sliding picture windows open up to a private terrace with a view of the sea. The Junior Suites and Deluxe Suites have four-poster beds, and come equipped with additional spaces such as a lounge area and

THIS PAGE (FROM TOP): Take a refreshing dip in the pool; facing the sea, the breezy Deluxe Suite has a laid-back ambience, enhanced by its soft and neutral colour tones.

OPPOSITE (CLOCKWISE FROM LEFT): At sunset, the entrance looks mesmerising under the lilac sky; al fresco dining with a twist at the Beachside Pavillion; Casa del Mar is known for its warm welcome and hospitality.

A home by the sea...

rooms
34

food
The Dining Room: Mediterranean and Malaysian

drink
Pool Bar • The Wine and Cigar Room

features
pool • spa • fitness centre • water sports

nearby
Kuah • Pantai Cenang Beach

contact
Jalan Pantai Cenang, 07000 Mukim
Kedawang, Langkawi, Kedah •
telephone: +60.4.955 2388 •
facsimile: +60.4.955 2228 •
email: info@casadelmar-langkawi.com •
website: www.casadelmar-langkawi.com

a dressing room. Sparkling white floors, cream cushions and the white, silky drapes hanging from the four-poster beds provide a vivid contrast to the rich, wooden furniture. All have sea views.

And for those who are not fans of isolation, no matter how beautiful the island, it's good to know that Casa del Mar is just a 10-minute drive from Langkawi International Airport and near Kuah, a quaint town where one can observe day-to-day life on the island.

Where dining is concerned, guests can enjoy Asian and Western cuisine from the hotel's kitchens—a beachside, moonlit dinner, or tuck in at the Dining Room amid Mediterranean-inspired fountains—or walk outside the boutique resort for some street food. In addition, one can also head towards The Wine and Cigar Room for fine liqueur and Havana's best cigars, such as Cuban Cohibas. And, there's always the poolside bar, where a game of spin-the-wheel can win you free cocktails.

Last but certainly not least, the resort, which dubs itself 'one of Langkawi's most personal hotels', has what is known as Casa del Mar's Castaway Picnic. For four hours, while marooned on an isolated island, guests can dine on smoked salmon and Moet et Chandon within a Bedouin tent carpeted with Persian rugs. Something the contestants of the reality television show *Survivor* must dream of during their trials.

cheong fatt tze mansion

The century-old Cheong Fatt Tze Mansion is called Penang's 'Blue Mansion' for its bright indigo-blue walls. Rescued from the perils of encroaching development, the 38-room building has been carefully restored to its former glory. In fact, so successful were restoration efforts that this Chinese courtyard mansion won the UNESCO Conservation Award for 2000.

The 3,066-sq-m (33,000-sq-ft) structure was built in the 1880s by Hakka tycoon Cheong Fatt Tze, who left his native China for Indonesia at the age of 16. The businessman made a fortune by trading, and expanded to Penang in 1886. Cheong became a powerful figure in trading and shipping and was even appointed Consul General for China, Mandarin of the Highest Order and Director of China's Railway.

Cheong Fatt Tze Mansion is a grand display of its eponymous builder's wealth and influence. The mansion, with its harmonious blend of Western and Oriental influences, is also a reflection of Cheong's fascination with various cultures. Light pours into the rooms from English art nouveau, stained glass windows, and Chinese calligraphy adorns trompe l'oeil timber beams. 'Chien Nien'— shards of colourful porcelain bowls imported from Fujian province in China—decorate some parts of the mansion. The doors are embossed with intricate gilded carvings of

THIS PAGE (FROM TOP): The water lily painting adds a serene touch to this sitting area; Cheong Fatt Tze Mansion is an architectural conservation wonder.

OPPOSITE (FROM TOP): Unwind on this verandah after a tour of the mansion; these trishaws evoke a bygone era.

flowers and other auspicious Chinese symbols. Graceful spiral staircases feature Scottish cast iron balusters with delicate floral patterns, contrasting well with the Cantonese timber lattices. The floors make an equally arresting sight with the sharp, geometrical patterns of terracotta tiles from China.

Cheong Fatt Tze Mansion has two parts: the main house, which is distinguished by the gables of the main roof, and two elegant side wings. Materials representing the feng shui elements of metal, timber, water, fire and earth are all present in the main hall. The rooms upstairs are fronted by a wood-panelled verandah which is shaded from the sun by heavy shutters made from tropical wood. Bamboo chairs line the verandah, as if inviting one to sit down and enjoy the tropical evening.

At the heart of the mansion are five granite-covered courtyards. In one courtyard, two majestic wooden stairs frame a set of giant, beautifully carved folding doors. There are outdoor dining areas filled with teak or tropical wood furniture, tapestries and antiques. Guests can glimpse other parts of the mansion from the courtyard. The indigo-blue walls can be seen through one door, and the gardens outside through another.

The mansion has been dubbed the epitome of 'feng shui perfection'. This comes as no surprise since a man of Cheong Fatt Tze's stature would have employed a master geomancer to determine the proper alignment

of elements in his prized home to ensure good luck and good fortune. To illustrate: Cheong Fatt Tze Mansion is located 'off the dragon's back', which means that it is situated on a slope, facing the sea with its back to the hills.

Join a guided tour of Cheong Fatt Tze Mansion to experience Penang's vibrant and colourful past. Tours are scheduled at 11.00 am and 3.00 pm. Better yet, stay for a day or two at this 'heirloom with rooms'. Choose from any of the 16 beautifully decorated rooms which are allocated for guests' homestays, and wake up to enjoy a freshly prepared breakfast served al fresco in the central courtyard. Additionally, celebrate special occasions at Cheong Fatt Tze Mansion—the largest and most historically significant venue for events in Penang.

rooms
38

features
indigo-blue walls · granite-paved courtyards · stained glass windows · heritage tours · homestays

nearby
Penang City Hall and Town Hall · Khoo Kongsi · Victoria Memorial Clocktower · St George's Church · Goddess of Mercy Temple.

contact
14 Leith Street, 10200 George Town, Penang · telephone: +60.4.262 0006 · facsimile: +60.4.262 5289 · email: cftm@tm.net.my · website: www.cheongfatttzemansion.com

eastern + oriental hotel

THIS PAGE: *Admire the full splendour of a beach sunset.*

OPPOSITE (FROM TOP): *The rooms at E&O Hotel are sumptuously decorated and provide the best of modern comforts; fresh fruit and baked delights for a wonderful afternoon tea.*

'Like being transported back in time' is a feeling often evoked at the Eastern & Oriental Hotel. Fondly known as the Grande Dame of Penang, it has a sweeping seafront location on George Town's elegant esplanade. This hotel formerly played host to powerful colonial administrators and guests such as Rudyard Kipling and Noel Coward. On an island bearing the moniker Pearl of the Orient, this palatial, whitewashed structure is an authentic piece of colonial history and following a majestic refurbishment in 2001, more glorious than ever.

A connoisseur's choice with flamboyant Moorish minarets silhouetted against swaying avenues of palms, the charming E&O Hotel was originally opened in 1885 by Armenian brothers Martin, Tigran and Arshak Sarkies. The brothers' chain of ultra-premium hotels also included The Strand in Rangoon and Singapore's Raffles Hotel, hotels which reigned for decades as the British Empire's finest. An aura of colonial grandeur still permeates every aspect of this legendary hotel, with its intuitively helpful doormen dressed in colonial attire always on hand to offer genuine Malaysian hospitality.

At 256 m (840 ft), the E&O Hotel boasts the longest sea-facing frontage in the world. Appreciate its marvellous view over the busy Strait of Malacca while sipping a cocktail on the shaded terrace, or from the enticing pool adorned with floating jasmine petals. For exercise more strenuous than a leisurely lap in the pool, visit the Fitness Suite with its fully equipped gym, sauna and steam bath.

Set amid lush tropical gardens that are home to the oldest Java tree in Malaysia, the E&O Hotel is an exclusive, all-suite grand hotel and local heritage landmark. Having successfully redefined the elegance of its bygone days, its 101 apartment-sized suites now exude a timeless splendour, with classic colonial touches such as teak furnishings intertwined with every modern convenience. Ranging from 54 sq m (581 sq ft) to a roomy 600-sq-m (6,458-sq-ft) in size, suites at the

rooms
101

food
The 1885: contemporary • Verandah: local and international • Sarkies Corner: local and international • The Bakery

drink
Farquhar's Bar • The Deck • The Conservatory

features
outdoor pool • fitness suite • gym • sauna • steam bath • satellite TV • minibar • 24-hour butler service • florist • limousine • doctor on call

business
business centre • secretarial services • Internet • Grand Ballroom • private function rooms

nearby
George Town

contact
10 Lebuh Farquhar, 10200 Penang • telephone: +60.4.222 2000 • facsimile: +60.4.261 6333 • email: hotel-info@e-o-hotel.com • website: www.e-o-hotel.com

hotel are opulently appointed and boast either sea or city views. Their expansive bathrooms—styled in classic Victorian fashion—feature traditional claw and ball bathtubs and separate 'his' and 'her' basins. All suites offer round-the-clock butler service.

The E&O culinary experience is second to none, with each dining venue emanating its own distinctive ambience. Traditional in style though contemporary in appeal is The 1885 restaurant, elegantly decorated in muted tones of marble grey and silken mink. This is where wine lovers and gourmets will truly meet their match. To step back in time for a slice of colonial Malaya, opt for a perfectly poured pint of beer at the clubhouse-style Farquhar's Bar, or a warming coffee amid the gleaming wood panels of Sarkies Corner. The Deck and Verandah Bar are perfect for a little al fresco refreshment in the afternoons, whereas The Conservatory, tickled by tropical breezes beneath the Java tree, should be the first port of call for a pre-dinner pick-me-up.

From its vantage point overlooking the Strait of Malacca, George Town perches at the very crossroads between East and West. If seeking an old world hotel from which to experience this town's fascinating fusion of art, language and architecture—not to mention its myriad shops, cafés and clubs—then the E&O Hotel is an unparalleled first choice. It is hard to miss and hard to forget.

four seasons resort langkawi

THIS PAGE: Generously sized villas afford charming views of lush palm trees and the emerald sea.

OPPOSITE (FROM LEFT): Enjoy the Middle Eastern ambience and tropical cocktails at Rhu Bar; Moorish arches are prominent features of the resort.

Guests are forgiven for thinking that Four Seasons Resort Langkawi is all about big impressions. After all, imposing 5-m- (16-ft-) high Ayuthia laterite walls from Thailand greet them when they step into the resort. But there is more behind the rich, red walls—and guests will soon find that Four Seasons Resort Langkawi is more about intimate luxury that creates a truly lasting impression.

The resort is a confluence of Malay, Indian and Arabic architecture. Beautiful gardens can be spied from curvy, Moghul Indian-style windows at the lobby. Arabic geometric design can be seen on mirrors, skylights, closet doors and even air vents. The rooms are the ultimate experience of resort living, with their soaring ceilings, wide timber floors and large open

verandahs that provide fantastic views. The 20 Beach Villas are especially delightful, with the beach a step down from their decks. When one spies the sun setting over the horizon and casting the islands around Langkawi in shadow at any of these villas, one wonders no more why Four Seasons Resort Langkawi is a favourite honeymoon spot.

However, the pièce de résistance is the decadent, Turkish-inspired hammam baths. The bathrooms are bright and airy—with sunlight pouring through the skylights—and one can soak in a bathtub built into a large terrazzo niche. All villas and lower-level pavilions have isolated outdoor bathing and shower areas that provide guests with an experience akin to taking a bath under a gentle rainfall.

At the foot of the limestone cliff towering over the resort are six private spa bungalows which seem to float over tranquil ponds. Close to the spa is the Family Pool, with many small coves that allow for privacy. There is also a 55-m (180-ft) Quiet Pool surrounded by luxurious private cabanas.

Dining choices are plentiful at the resort. Enjoy Italian classics at Serai, or tuck into Thai, Chinese and Malay cuisine at Ikan-Ikan. Have a drink at Kafe Kelapa, or enjoy Turkish water pipes while lounging on the sofas at Rhu Bar.

The people behind Four Seasons Resort Langkawi are masters of resort living They certainly know the meaning of luxurious indulgence, and can always be expected to provide guests with an inimitable experience.

...a confluence of Malay, Indian and Arabic architecture.

rooms
68 pavilions • 23 villas

food
Serai: Italian • Ikan-Ikan: Southeast Asian •
Kafe Kelapa: Western and Asian

drink
Rhu Bar

features
gym • pools • tennis court • spa • retail gallery

nearby
Kilim Nature Park • Gunung Raya • Langkawi
Underwater World • Taman Lagenda • The
Craft Cultural Complex • Air Hangat Village •
Langkawi Cable Car

contact
Jalan Tanjung Rhu, 07000 Langkawi, Kedah •
telephone: +60.4.950 8888 •
facsimile: +60.4.950 8899 •
email: reservations.lan@fourseasons.com •
website: www.fourseasons.com/langkawi

japamala resorts

For a fashionably rustic Asian experience, head for the luxurious JapaMala Resorts on the southwestern coast of Tioman Island. Opened in 2003, this tranquil haven of ivory white beaches and turquoise waters is a glistening pearl dropped into the sea off Malaysia's eastern coast.

This unique boutique resort is more than a pretty façade. It has an environmental conscience too, and was sustainably built with an eye to the future and consideration for local communities. JapaMala's eco-friendly chalets and Sarang Villas are located within a protected marine park, harmoniously blending with the unparalleled beauty of their natural surroundings.

The finer things in life are all just waiting to be enjoyed here. From gourmet cuisine to exploring the subterranean treasures at its dive sites, this resort has it all. The stunning offshore reefs are perfect for mini snorkelling adventures to break up the endless bouts of dedicated sun worshipping. JapaMala has even coined the phrase Jungle Luxe, as guests not only get to enjoy five-star amenities, they can also head out for a lazy afternoon's beachcombing, canyoning or jungle trekking.

On arrival, guests are asked which aromatic scents they would prefer in their villas at night—a sign of the indulgent pampering to come. Characterised by friendly staff and a traditional village-style charm, JapaMala belongs to the internationally reputed Relais & Chateaux group, having met their '5C' gold standard for a resort with great character, calm, charm, courtesy and cuisine. The resort was also rated among the 'World's Top 10 Ultra Boutique Resorts' by luxury travel site globorati.com—the only Malaysian hotel selected.

THIS PAGE (FROM TOP): The plunge pool at Sarang Villa; Mandi-Mandi is a restaurant built on stilts 100 m (328 ft) away from the beachfront; guests can look forward to a range of activities on the pristine white beach.

OPPOSITE (FROM TOP): The wide dining space at Tamarind Terrace exudes Asian elegance; take in breathtaking views of the South China Sea from the Seacliff Chalet.

Of the personalised accommodation, no two are the same. There are fans and air-conditioning to keep humidity at bay, large beds in which to curl up and an extensive DVD library. The bathrooms are sparkling and generously proportioned. Handcrafted finishing touches such as beach pebbles set into the surfaces further add to the tropical ambience of these cool, wooden retreats.

The nature-inspired interiors of the villas feature vibrant Asian decorations. Lavish yet simple, fashionable yet rustic, these secluded escapes will appeal to those who want to get away from the frenetic pace of urban life while taking their home comforts with them. Honeymooners and couples will enjoy the exotic plunge pool villas, with a private jacuzzi on the cool, shaded sundeck.

JapaMala is perhaps best known for its award-winning Tamarind Terrace, the open-to-nature restaurant perched on Tioman Island's pristine, jungle-fringed beachfront. Thai, Indochinese and traditional Malay cuisine are served here, with the South China Sea as backdrop. This restaurant offers warm service, an intimate ambience and the gentle burbling of adjacent natural springs as its relaxing natural soundtrack.

For the ultimate indulgence, reserve a Tioman Island Experience at Samadhi Spa. This wellness centre, with cliff-perched jacuzzis and sea-view treatment rooms, is the personification of relaxation and rejuvenation, bringing peace to mind, body and soul.

JapaMala. It's not just a place. It's a state of mind.

rooms
12

food
Tamarind Terrace: Thai, Indochinese and Malay • Mandi-Mandi Restaurant: international and Italian

drink
extensive wine list

features
minibar • jacuzzi • massage • Samadhi Spa • wellness centre • city shuttle service • snorkelling • kayaking

nearby
Mukut Waterfalls • Coral Island • Sepoy Rock • Bahara Island • Tulai Island • Tiger Reef • Chebeh Island

contact
Kampung Lanting
86800 Pulau Tioman, Pahang •
telephone: +60.9.419 7777 •
facsimile: 60.9.419 7979 •
email: info@japamalaresorts.com •
website: www.japamalaresorts.com

pangkor laut resort

Off the west coast of Malaysia lies the privately owned island, Pangkor Laut, home to one of the most luxurious resorts in the world. Since its creation in the 1990s, the Pangkor Laut Resort has earned much praise from holidaymakers and critics alike. It is also a favourite retreat for celebrities, including the late Italian tenor Luciano Pavarotti—who has a suite in the resort named after him— and actress Joan Collins.

Occupying a secluded spot in the heart of an ancient tropical forest, it is not difficult to see why the resort is highly rated among discerning travellers looking for some peace and tranquillity, not to mention that it is a haven for spa enthusiasts. The resort's Spa Village is fully equipped with treatment pavilions and offers an impressive range of treatments from around the region.

When guests arrive at the jetty, they are greeted by the enchanting villas that are held above the turquoise waters on wooden stilts. Guests will also be captivated by the sight of the colourful watercraft anchored at the yacht marina that fronts the reception area.

rooms
142

food
Fisherman's Cove: Italian, Western and seafood •
Uncle Lim's Kitchen: Hock Chew and Nonya •
Royal Bay Beach Club: fusion • Chapman's Bar:
traditional and seafood • Jamu Bar: Japanese •
The Straits: Southeast Asian • Feast Village:
Asia-Pacific cuisine

drink
Chapman's Bar

features
Spa Village • sauna • Jim Thompson Boutique •
Spa Boutique • pools • Kazbah boutique •
batik hut • library • conference hall •
tennis courts • fitness centre • squash court •
catamaran sailing • wind surfing • kayaking •
water skiing

nearby
Pangkor Island • Pangkor Forest Reserve •
Pasir Giam Beach

contact
Pangkor Laut Island, 32200 Lumut, Perak •
telephone: +60.5.699 1100 •
facsimile: +60.5.699 1200 •
email: travelcentre@ytlhotels.com.my •
website: www.pangkorlautresort.com

The décor at Pangkor Laut is tropical chic. The lap pool is fringed by lush tropical plants; gleaming hardwood floors and rich, brown furniture give the interior a cosy ambience. If guests want a quiet reading corner, or to simply while away a lazy afternoon, they can head to the four small pavilions that are furnished with silk cushions, bolsters and views of lush greenery.

The accommodation here is just as indulgent. Guests of the Sea and Spa Villas, and the Purnama and Suria Suites, sleep with the sound of waves lapping beneath their villas. The Hill Villas are perched on a hillside surrounded by the rainforest, which gives the rooms a magnificent view of the sea and the resort's tropical gardens. Taking a bath in the Hill Villas is an experience on its own, as private courtyards—with a huge bathtub—open out to the rainforest.

The Beach Villas are but a few steps away from the beach, while the double-storey Garden Villas are set right in the heart of the tropical gardens. The two-bedroom Pavarotti Suite—where the tenor stayed during his performance at the resort—is surely one of the highlights of the resort, which is hardly surprising. Star factor aside, the suite has a spacious balcony, big lounge area and open-roofed bathroom with breathtaking views of the sea and the rainforest.

Walk into Pangkor Laut Resort, and one retreats from the frenetic pace of urban life into a peaceful sanctuary.

tanjong jara resort

'Unmistakably Malay', so goes the tagline for Tanjong Jara Resort, located on the shores of Terengganu, on the east coast of Malaysia. One may add that the Tanjong Jara Resort is also unmistakably luxurious, as it was designed to reflect the grandeur of traditional Malay palaces.

The resort's elegantly crafted and leisure-filled abodes look like 17th-century Malay istanas (palaces). Given that such special attention was paid to the creation of the building, it is not difficult to see why Tanjong Jara Resort won the coveted Aga Khan Award for Architecture.

The beauty of these Malay palaces is enhanced by its stunning natural surroundings. The scenery is captivating and enchanting: the South China Sea's emerald waters sparkle in the sunset, palm leaves sway and rustle in the breeze, and the rainforest teems with wildlife. The water features that can be found around the resort—such as the sparkling tranquillity pools—simply lull guests into a state of zen.

Certainly, Tanjong Jara Resort is more than just architecture and natural beauty. Thanks to the gentle Malay traditions of service and hospitality, guests are made to

THIS PAGE: The peaceful sanctuary of Tanjong Jara Resort beckons.

OPPOSITE: With soft lighting and classic décor, the resort exudes warmth and style.

feel like sultans and sultanahs. When guests first step foot into the resort, they are welcomed with the resort's famed Roselle drink, made from the extract of the eponymous plant's dark red flower calyces, which are said to have unique healing powers.

Indeed, the Roselle Experience is one of the highlight treatments at the Spa Village Tanjong Jara. It begins with a massage, where oil made from a blend of Roselle, ginger, nutmeg, galangal and karoteno oil is rubbed on the body. Creamy Roselle scrub is then used to exfoliate and cleanse the skin. And the treatment ends with a cup of steaming Roselle tea served to the thoroughly pampered guest.

It is not surprising that the Spa Village takes good care of guests' well-being. After all, one of Tanjong Jara's main objectives is to rejuvenate both body and spirit. In fact the resort's philosophy revolves around the Malay concept of suci murni, which puts an emphasis on the purity of spirit, health and well-being.

The spa's therapy centre is found in the midst of lush, tropical gardens and tranquil pools. Here, guests can experience the restorative Malay treatments that have been handed down from generation to generation for more than a thousand years. Intriguingly, these treatments originated from the days of the Malacca Sultanate, when Malacca was a thriving port where Malay, Arab, Indian and Chinese merchants mingled freely. The Spa

For maximum luxury, there's the 176-sq-m (1,894-sq-ft) Anjung Suite, the resort's premier suite. The suite, which looks like a traditional home in a fishing village, overlooks the river that runs through the resort and into the South China Sea. The living room is furnished with comfortable sofas, while a dining hall, a bar and powder room make up the best of modern comforts, not to mention a sunken bath that will soak up one's worries and drive them away. Guests can also choose to while their afternoon away on the king-sized bed.

The doors and windows of the Anjung Room open out to a canopied terrace, and it has a private garden with a sunken outdoor bath, the perfect spot to soak in a floral bath. The other rooms are just as impressive. The Serambi Room has a partially covered verandah, while the Bumbung Room provides breathtaking views of the sea and gardens.

Certainly, guests will want to venture out of the comforts of their luxurious rooms to discover the rugged terrain around the resort, and they won't be short of options. One can either take a jaunt down the Marang River or trek to one of Southeast Asia's highest waterfalls, the Cemerung.

Tanjong Jara also offers splendid opportunities for snorkelling and scuba diving at Tenggol Island, which is just 45 minutes away from the resort on a speedboat. Unspoilt coral gardens and rare species of marine life guarantee a memorable underwater experience for beginners and

Village offers a wide range of programmes, from Mandi Bunga for women to luxuriate in a floral bath, to Urutan Panglima for men. And as icing on the cake, guests are given a memento—a batik sarong—at the end of a treatment at the Spa Village.

The guestrooms at the resort are equally indulgent, offering spectacular views of both the landscaped tropical gardens and the blue sea. A cosy ambience fills the rooms, as the warm colours of the timber flooring and furniture are complemented by cushions and drapes made from exquisite local materials.

THIS PAGE: Surrounded by lush tropical beauty, the richly-furnished rooms ensure a relaxing stay for guests.

OPPOSITE (FROM TOP): There is no lack of dining options at Tanjong Jara Resort; enjoy a candlelit dinner under the night sky.

experienced divers alike. Diving equipment may be rented from the Water Sports Centre, and guests can obtain a PADI Open Water Diver licence as part of their holiday.

Wining and dining at Tanjong Jara Resort is something to relish as the resort's surroundings often play a part in enhancing the entire experience. Di Atas Sungei (Malay for 'above the river') is one such example. The restaurant, which serves Malaysian cuisine, has a dark timber balcony that literally sits above a river which flows into the South China Sea. A huge Ketapang tree hovers over the restaurant, providing welcome shade for guests who are often there for breakfast, as well as dinner.

At the Teratai Terrace, located beside the free-form pool with a view of the sea, diners will welcome the cool breeze from the sea as they enjoy a bubbling steamboat dinner.

Nelayan (Fisherman) is another superb dining option, serving a variety of local and Western light meals. The resort has its own fishermen to bring back the catch for dinner, so guests get to feast on the freshest of seafood at Nelayan, amid bamboo torches flickering in the calm sea breeze and the gentle lapping of waves.

More than just rejuvenating mind and body, Tanjong Jara Resort is a fusion of nature, Malay culture and impeccable service, the ideal retreat for the discerning traveller.

rooms
99

food
Di Atas Sungei: Malaysian • The Nelayan: local and seafood • Teratai Terrace: steamboat dinner

drink
Teratai Terrace • Nelayan Lounge

features
culinary classes • bicycle tour • jungle trekking • golf • river cruises • snorkelling • diving

nearby
Marang River • Cemerung Waterfall • Tenggol Island • Tasik Puteri Golf Club • Dungun • Kuala Terengganu Floating Mosque

contact
Batu 8, off Jalan Dungun 23000 Dungun, Terengganu • telephone: +60.9.845 1100 • facsimile: +60.9.845 1200 • email: tjara@ytlhotels.com.my • website: www.tanjongjararesort.com

the andaman langkawi

Mother Nature enjoys great prominence at The Andaman. The luxury resort, located on the legend-filled island of Langkawi off the coast of Kedah, takes every opportunity to let nature in. Rooms are bathed in the warm sunlight that streams through generous windows and balconies. Wooden shutters open to a panoramic view of the rainforest and the Andaman Sea, and in some parts of the resort, walls are folded away to create open spaces to let the balmy sea air in.

Langkawi's rich, tropical forest—teeming with wildlife—surrounds the resort, so it is not unusual to spot a monkey on a tree branch from a room window, or hear the songs of tropical birds in the mornings.

At the resort, contemporary architecture is juxtaposed with classical Malay design. While the old world charm of a quaint Malay village is palpable, guests are not deprived of modern sensibilities, as every room is equipped with the latest amenities. The rooms are tastefully decorated with the warm colours of earthy, traditional wooden furniture, complementing well with the modern fixtures and décor. The Lanai Rooms on the first floor come with sunning decks—a great spot to get a tan. Ultimate luxury can be found in the suites, which come with the best of modern comforts, complete with one bedroom, a separate living area, spacious balcony and a private bar.

THIS PAGE (FROM TOP):Furnished like a traditional Malay home, The Gulai House offers fine dining in the most authentic style; a relaxing swim in the impressive pool beckons.

OPPOSITE (FROM TOP): Take in the breathtaking view of the Andaman Sea in the spacious Executive Suite; enjoy traditional dining in the private tatami rooms of The Japanese Restaurant.

Wooden shutters open to a panoramic view of the rainforest and the Andaman sea...

rooms
187

food
The Gulai House: Malay and Indian •
The Japanese Restaurant: Japanese •
The Restaurant: Asian and continental •
The Poolside BBQ Terrace: barbeque buffet

drink
Lobby Lounge • The Beach Bar •
The Poolside Terrace

features
satellite TV • gym • limousine • car rental •
babysitter on request • tennis courts • pool •
billiard and games room • library •
18-hole championship golf course

business
business centre

nearby
Telaga Tujuh • Pulau Dayang Bunting •
Makam Mahsuri • Telaga Air Hangat •
Gua Cerita •Pantai Pasir Hitam

contact
Jalan Teluk Datai, PO Box 94
07000 Langkawi, Kedah •
telephone: +60.4.959.1088 •
facsimile: +60.4.959.1168 •
email: andaman@ghmhotels.com •
website: www.theandaman.com

The Andaman's relaxation centre, The Spa, takes full advantage of its stunning surroundings. Located high above the ground next to the tree tops, its open-air, duplex-style Rainforest Villas provide the perfect spot to indulge in a warm bath sprinkled with fragrant flowers while admiring the unobstructed view of the rolling hills beyond the sea. The Sari Villa, a private villa with a large jacuzzi, relaxation terrace and garden shower, offers a more private rejuvenation session.

There are several recreational options available. Guests may tee off at the 18-hole championship golf course nearby, enjoy exclusive use of the beach, or simply take a leisurely swim in the organic-shaped pool. In addition, Langkawi's historic and myth-laced attractions such as Makam Mahsuri and the black beach of Pantai Pasir Hitam are just a short drive away.

When it comes to cuisine, guests are spoilt for choice with the many restaurants and 24-hour room service the resort provides. Located 300 m (984 ft) away from the main building and right in the midst of the rainforest, The Gulai House combines culture and cuisine to give dinners an exotic twist—fine Malay and Indian cuisine is served in a setting akin to a traditional Malay home.

The Andaman is a peaceful oasis, an exquisite resort where guests get to enjoy the warmth of the tropics, the sea breeze and the white, sandy beaches of Datai Bay at the same time.

the datai langkawi

Nothing says 'resort experience' quite like The Datai, which is located on Kedah's Langkawi Island. Zen-like calm permeates the resort, surrounded by a rainforest and fronted by a secluded white, sandy beach facing the cerulean waters of the Andaman Sea.

The Datai was built to complement the surrounding tropical rainforest, which is dramatic and full of life. If visitors are lucky, they can even spot a flying squirrel gliding from tree to tree, or spy a sea eagle soaring in the sky above. Langkawi, after all, is the fusion of two Malay words: helang (eagle) and kawi (reddish brown eagle), and the island is thus named after these majestic bird species.

When guests enter the lobby, they are greeted by two giant horse statues that stand guard from their position on the pedestal. The high ceiling, on the other hand, gives one the feeling of being in an ancient palace of a sultan.

The rooms are just as impressive. Floor-to-ceiling windows let in fresh, salty air from the sea and allow guests to enjoy the view of the rainforest and sparkling blue sea. Wooden timber floors give the rooms warmth, which is complemented by the strong, simple shapes of the furniture.

For guests who desire a more private retreat, there are the Pool Villas. Nestled in the midst of the vibrant flora of the rainforest, these villas may look like kampung houses on the outside, but once inside, one will be surrounded by modern luxuries, the highlight being the private plunge pool. There is even a private deck with a daybed for a little meditation or a quiet read.

The Datai underwent a revamp recently, upgrading its villas to Superior Villas, which are much larger and equipped with the latest modern comforts such as LCD flat-screen TV, DVD player, Bose CD sound system and a

THIS PAGE (FROM TOP): Lush greenery surrounds the resort; enjoy both Western and local cuisine in the modern interior of The Dining Room; The Pavilion offers the ideal setting for a relaxing meal.

OPPOSITE (FROM TOP): The Superior Villas are spacious, and exude warmth and a tropical feel; a private plunge pool awaits guests residing in the Pool Villa.

rooms
112

food
The Pavilion: Thai • The Dining Room: Western and local • The Beach Club: local, seafood, Southeast Asian, Italian, Mediterranean

drink
Lobby Lounge

features
health club with gym • massage • sauna • hot and cold plunge baths • limousine • car rental • duty-free boutique • library • babysitter on request • tennis courts • pools • jungle trekking • mountain bikes

nearby
18-hole championship Datai Bay Golf Course • Pulau Dayang Bunting • Lake of the Pregnant Maiden • Telaga Tujuh (The Seven Wells)

contact
Jalan Teluk Datai, 07000 Langkawi, Kedah • telephone: +60.4.959 2500 • facsimile: +60.4.959 2600 • email: datai@ghmhotels.com • website: www.langkawi-resorts.com/datailk

Lavazza coffee machine. A spacious bathroom doubles up as a personal spa, providing guests with a rain shower and twin terrazzo vanities, among other amenities.

The End Suites and Corner Suites were renovated as well, giving these spacious suites—complete with dining and living room areas, and individual bedrooms with ensuite bathrooms—a new look. The same was done for the resort's 21 Deluxe Rooms.

Certainly, The Datai offers more than just superb rooms. The Spa, which has a wide range of services, ensures a rejuvenating spa experience for guests with treatments like the Ayurvedic Abhyanga massage and the 50-minute Sundari facial.

Alternatively, soak in the beauty of Mother Nature by kayaking around the coastline, or get on a mountain bike to explore the rustic beauty of Langkawi island.

Guests can also choose to enjoy the peace and tranquillity in the relaxing ambience of the restaurants. The Pavilion, set high in the canopy of the rainforest, serves authentic Thai food in an al fresco setting. Offering a gorgeous view of the sea as diners sample one of its themed dinners, The Beach Club provides the ideal venue for some romantic dining by the sea.

An oasis of serenity in the heart of a tropical rainforest, The Datai is one holiday hideaway that one shouldn't miss.

indulgence restaurant + living

The city of Ipoh remains an enigma, with its greater population of over 1 million people a magnet to those with relatives residing there, bolstered by travellers on the crossroads between Penang and Kuala Lumpur.

Indulgence Restaurant & Living is an oasis of urbanity in the timeless rural desert of Ipoh. Set in a splendid 1940s colonial mansion amid stately grounds in the heart of Ipoh, one is transported to Mediterranean Provence with the bright and breezy décor and spacious, sunlit rooms.

Chef proprietor Julie Song imparts a refreshing cosmopolitanism and lack of pretence with a touch of Melbourne café culture and sophistication augmented by her innovative cooking talents. Indulgence sets many precedents not only in Ipoh, but in all of Malaysia in terms of dining concept, top quality local and imported produce and modern European influenced cuisine.

With a vast menu, Indulgence caters to an eclectic clientele, whether it is for breakfast, brunch, lunch, afternoon tea, dinner or supper. Guests can drop in any time for one of Malaysia's best espresso coffees, or perhaps some dessert from Julie's extensive repertoire of sweets. Another speciality is a creative and tantalising selection of salads.

Within an extensive range of wines chosen with expertise and tailored to the cuisine, one will also be tempted by rare

THIS PAGE (FROM TOP): Rich ethnic themes dominate the décor of all guestrooms at Indulgence Restaurant & Living; May-Suet is one of six individually designed rooms.

OPPOSITE (FROM TOP): Sublime meals are an everyday experience at the restaurant; the food at Indulgence pleases the eye and the palate.

...an oasis of urbanity in the timeless rural desert of Ipoh.

rooms
2 themed suites • 4 themed deluxe rooms

seats
main dining: 120 • Alessandria room: 20 •
Krystal room: 8 • Parlour: 40

food
modern European

drink
extensive wine list

features
boutique hotel

nearby
city centre • Parkson Grand mall

contact
14 Jalan Raja Dihilir, 30350 Ipoh, Perak •
telephone: +60.5.255 7051 •
facsimile: +60.5.242 6297 •
email: indulge@indulgencerestaurant.com •
website: www.indulgencerestaurant.com

and premium labels made by artisan producers from the outstanding wine-growing regions of the world.

Indulgence is Perak's pre-eminent venue for private functions suitable for any occasion—be it an exclusive degustation menu or a cosy private dining room for a small party, or buffet for a bigger event.

Confined to basic, three-star hotels, refined accommodation in Ipoh has been non-existent—until the opening of the restaurant's hotel that is. Indeed, Indulgence Living breaks new ground in Malaysia with its avant-garde boutique luxury hotel concept.

The second floor of the restaurant houses six rooms that are exquisitely decorated and painstakingly designed, each with a different theme and extravagant furnishings. There are two suites, the romantic Beverly with an English country setting, and Tzarrah with its striking Moroccan colours and textures. The four deluxe rooms comprise Ildi, contemporary in its modern elegance yet audacious with its glossy colours; May-Suet, Chinoiserie with a nostalgic feel of old Shanghai; Kinnaree, Thai theme resonating with silks and gold leaf; and Guilianna, Italian grandeur with plush avant-garde textiles.

This alone is reason to visit Ipoh more than once a year, escaping from the hustle and bustle of city life to luxuriate in Indulgence Restaurant & Living, and perhaps take in the traditional charms of old Ipoh at the same time.

eastmalaysia

PHILIPPINES

Sulu S

South China Sea

P. Balambangan *P. Banggi*

Tanjung Simpang
Mengayau
○ Kudat

P. Malawali

P. Jambongan

○ **Pitas**

P. Kalampunian

• Turtle Islands
National Park

The Kudat Riviera ‹
Nexus Resort Karambunai ‹
@mosphere Modern Dining ‹
Touchdown Luxury Yacht + Helicopter Charters ‹
The English Tea House + Restaurant ‹

▲ *Gunung*
4095 *Kinabalu*

Kota Kinabalu ○

○ **Ranau**

○ Sandakan

○ Papar

SABAH

○ **Beaufort**

Gunung
2649 *Trus Madi*

Labuan ◉

○ **Keningau**

Lahad Datu ○

P. Sakar

✛ *Brunei*
Bay

○ **Melalap**
○ **Tenom**

○ T

○ **Lawas**

○ **Tomani**

P. Timbun Mc

B R U N E I

○ **Sapulut**

○ Semp

Tanjung Baram

Kalabakan ○

Miri ○

○ **Tawau**

✛

Celebes

Suai ○

• Gunung Mulu National Park

✛ 2371
Gunung
Mulu

Bintulu ○
✛

Balingian ○

Banjaran Tama Abu

Banjaran Witti

Banjaran

Sea

Oya ○

○ **Belaga**

Tanjung Sirik

1465
▲
Bukit
Batu
Bora

SARAWAK

✛
Sibu ○

Pegunungan Hose

Sarikei ○

Borneo

Pegunungan Kapuas Hulu

○ **Sematan**

1281
▲
Bukit
Lomjak

Kuching
✈

Semenggoh
Wildlife Centre
Bandar Sri Aman ○

I N D O N E S I A

Legend

— Main R
⊕ Air
✛ Dome
Airp
○ L

▓ 3000-400
▓ 2000-300
▓ 1000-200
▓ 500-100
▓ 200-50

0 km   60   120   18

east malaysia

from wild to mild

Located on the island of Borneo, East Malaysia comprises the states of Sabah and Sarawak, along with the federal territory of Labuan. The tiny oil-rich Sultanate of Brunei is sandwiched in the middle. The gulf between East and West Malaysia is greater than the 644 km (400 miles) of ocean that separates them.

The history of Sabah and Sarawak is different from that of the peninsula. British control was more direct, whether through the ruling dynasty of Brooke Rajahs in Sarawak or the British North Borneo Company, which administered the territory now called Sabah. The heads of state are now governors rather than sultans.

The ethnic mix is also different from the peninsula. The majority in both Sabah and Sarawak are indigenous tribes, followed by

the Chinese, Malays and Indians. The tribal tradition is a matter of considerable pride and occasional irreverence. When a cocktail called a 'headhunter' is served in a head-shaped vessel, it is hard to know how seriously to take it. In other cases, the warfaring past is the essence of Bornean identity. These days, tribal chiefs often live in urban communities but are still given a lot of respect, especially the 'paramount chiefs'. The vestiges of a raw, tribal aura that come with Borneo's countless indigenous communities have helped to create events such as the Borneo International Tattoo Convention and the Rainforest World Music Festival, which attract participants from around the world.

References to the past may be everywhere in East Malaysia, but it is a forward-looking place with most of the amenities that can be found in the peninsula. The towns tend to be smaller and the capital cities retain a feel that is friendly and almost provincial. Both cities are expanding rapidly. Kuching is still the largest in East Malaysia, with a population of 600,000; Kota Kinabalu is catching up fast.

Not only are East Malaysian towns generally small, there are also far fewer of them. It is nature that rules in Borneo, land of the eco-tourist. Being the third largest island in the world,

THIS PAGE: A bird's eye view of a massive squatter colony in the city of Sandakan, Sabah.

PAGE 160: Sarawak and Sabah are home to the swiftlets that create one of the most expensive Chinese delicacies. Bird's nests are collected in perilous fashion from the caves where the swiftlets congregate.

with endless vistas of primary rainforest, the attractions are generally green. There are boat trips along tranquil jungle rivers, and other water activities such as white-water rafting. One can also trek up Malaysia's highest mountain, Kinabalu (4,095 m or 13,435 ft), or explore deep caves in which some of man's oldest ancestors made their homes.

Both states have a wide variety of wildlife, from soaring hornbills to the orang utans in the Sepilok Orangutan Rehabilitation Centre. There is also the world's largest and least-fragrant flower—the Rafflesia, named in honour of the ubiquitous Sir Stamford Raffles, who was a member of the expedition that discovered it. Of the two states, Sarawak is the larger and more densely forested; Sabah's greatest asset is the sea. Scuba diving in areas of the east coast such as Mabul, Kapalai and Sipadan is ranked among the best in the world and was extravagantly praised by Jacques Cousteau, the renowned French marine explorer and ecologist. The seafood is also exceptional. Sabah's coastline is dotted with restaurants on stilts that serve the freshest and most reasonably priced fish and crustaceans in Malaysia, a country that has an insatiable passion for 'fruits of the sea'.

different sides to island life

Most of the population of East Malaysia is concentrated near the coast. Before transport and communications improved in the 20th century, the inland inhabitants were hardy hill tribes and traders eager to exploit the natural riches of Borneo. This was an island which had many of the resources most admired by the greatest Asian power of the past; China was relentless in its pursuit of exotic luxuries such as camphor, rattan, hornbill casque and bird's nest, which were available almost nowhere else. In exchange, the island's natives received beads and large earthenware jars that are still revered as their most precious heirlooms.

THIS PAGE: A waterfall in the Lambir Hills National Park, Sarawak.

OPPOSITE (FROM LEFT): Giant caves are the main attraction at Gunung Mulu National Park, which is also home to an astonishing diversity of plant and animal life; the Rhinoceros Hornbill is one of Borneo's largest birds and an emblem of the state of Sarawak.

...take advantage of the astonishingly clear blue seas of Sabah.

The number of authentic longhouses has inevitably declined with growing commercial opportunities in coastal towns. The amount of rainforest has also shrunk; timber remains one of the cornerstones of the East Malaysian economy. Towns like Sibu in Sarawak have been built almost entirely on money from this business and have spawned some of Malaysia's richest tycoons. These are mostly from the Foochow community and include newspaper magnate Tan Sri Tiong Hiew King.

East Malaysian towns have expanded without losing much of their original charm. Kuching has one of Asia's loveliest and least-spoilt river frontages, overlooking a palace and other buildings from the era of the Brooke dynasty. In the same vicinity is Jalan Main Bazaar. This road is filled with shophouses from a century ago, often selling similarly antiquated wares. Among the opportunities for art collectors is the small stock of Bornean carvings and textiles that have not already been exported to the West. This is a field of tribal art with as much technical mastery as Africa or Oceania, but available at considerably lower prices. However, one should beware of modern imitations.

Shopping used to be a low priority for visitors to East Malaysia. This is changing. In recent years, numerous malls have been built and the old shophouses have become increasingly redundant. For the moment, however, this is still a place for quiet relaxation. There are many five-star resorts, most of them on the coast of Sabah. Locations such as Nexus Karambunai, Shangri-La's Tanjung Aru, Rasa Ria resorts and the Sutera Harbour Resort take advantage of the astonishingly clear blue seas of Sabah. Sarawak's coastline, having more estuaries, is closer to a muddy brown colour.

Golf is another of Borneo's attractions, creating a different sort of green awareness among the locals and enthusiasts from as far away as Japan and Korea. The majority of East Malaysia's top courses are in Sabah; some are of championship standard and almost all have the attraction of views onto the clear blue waters for which the state is famed. Many of the courses are as new as the massive increase in tourism that the state has experienced in recent years. However, trees grow fast in this part of the world and the landscaping has matured attractively in a very short time. Sabah, in particular, is becoming a haven for retirees and second-home owners from the most affluent corners of Asia. An enormous amount of property development has taken place in the more scenic parts of Sabah but this has not stopped prices going up.

As with every part of Malaysia, Sabah and Sarawak provide an enticing picture of stability. There are few tensions and the people are perhaps even friendlier to visitors than elsewhere in the country.

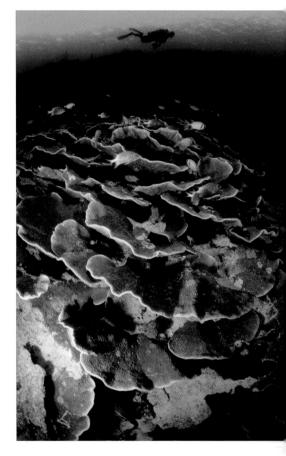

THIS PAGE: *Lettuce corals and squirrelfish can be spotted in the sparkling clear waters off the east coast of Borneo.*

OPPOSITE: *Sipadan Island is among the most popular diving spots in the region.*

PAGE 168: *The Salak River in Sarawak winds its way through coastal mangrove, swamps and forests.*

nexus resort karambunai

Awarded the coveted Gold Award by Virgin Holidays in 2006 and a frequent entrant to Top Ten luxury lists the world over, Nexus Resort Karambunai is Sabah's premier beach and golfing destination. Caressing 6 km (4 miles) of blinding white sands on its own private peninsula, this resort is enveloped on all sides by the piercing blue waters of the South China Sea.

At the entrance, this haven of rest and relaxation welcomes guests beneath a striking, high pointed wood-tiled roof, inspired by indigenous Bajau designs. Once inside, Nexus Resort Karambunai's luxury suites and villas speckle the landscaped hillsides among hectares of rich green foliage and tropical plants. Its harmonious, low-level buildings are naturally intersected by the

cyan waters of meandering inlets and pristine lagoons, with a million-year-old forest forming the backdrop to this picturesque scene.

Spacious and secluded, Nexus Resort Karambunai is ideal for honeymooning couples and keen sportsmen alike. Hop on a golf buggy and within minutes, the superb par-72, 18-hole course comes into view, along with a driving range and putting green. With a challenging, Ronald Fream-designed course that offers magnificent ocean views, it is no wonder that Nexus Resort Karambunai was recently voted Malaysia's Top Golf Resort at the World Travel Awards.

The accommodation at this charming resort is equally impressive. The elegant suites are coloured with tones from a restful, warming palette, and feature solid, handcrafted wood furnishings. Each boasts its own private balcony, with designer amenities scattered at every opportunity, along with finishing touches like luxuriant robes and coffee-making facilities.

Stretching out along Frangipani Cove, each Executive Ocean Room has a panoramic view that truly does justice to its name. Nearby, the Deluxe Borneo Suites are set amid swaying palm trees and bougainvillea blooms, with quaint garden pathways winding peacefully in between. Each room is designed to impress with its sea- or garden-facing terrace or balcony. Several rooms boast private pools or patios for impromptu parties and candlelit dinners.

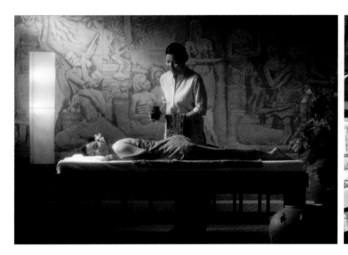

THIS PAGE (FROM LEFT): *Relax and enjoy a range of rejuvenating treatments at Borneo Spa; this Royal Villa master bedroom inspires with its luxurious décor.*

OPPOSITE (FROM LEFT): *Look forward to an array of activities at the beach; savour delectable local cuisine and the freshest of seafood at The Kingfisher.*

For the ultimate Nexus Resort Karambunai experience, the Luxury Villas provide the answer. These Royal and Presidential Villas offer 300 sq m (3,229 sq ft) of exquisitely designed modern comfort and convenience, veiled by private gardens for utmost privacy, stretching down to the South China Sea.

The tranquil oasis that is the Borneo Spa exists to pamper those preferring outside help to attain that elusive state of pure, unadulterated bliss. In-room visits are particularly popular, with artful masseuses using the spa's signature essential oils to bring their soothing skills directly to guests' doorsteps. For a more luxurious experience, guests can head to the jacuzzi, steam bath or sauna at the spa itself. If toning while tanning is all important, simply opt for a private massage in a private beachfront cabana, to maximise sun exposure.

Even though the sea is an ever-present temptation, Nexus Resort Karambunai has nonetheless created three free-form pools within its gardens. For a refreshing cocktail or juice in between leisurely laps, Splashes, the poolside bar, will offer a little pick-me-up. Those seeking an adrenaline rush will welcome the adjacent Karambunai Lagoon Park, with its plethora of sun-soaked activities that include water skiing, jet skiing, kayaking and sport fishing. Guests can also head to the beachfront for some horseback riding, beach volleyball, cycling or a nature walk.

The wining and dining possibilities at the resort are diverse enough to excite any palate, with no fewer than eight bars and restaurants to select from. The comfortable Horizon Lounge features plump cushions on oversized rattan chairs, ideal to sink into with a refreshing cup of afternoon tea. The Penyu

Restaurant is just a stone's throw away, offering a tantalising array of international and local cuisine. For dim sum or aromatic Cantonese dishes prepared in a flash, step into the vibrant red interior of Noble House. The Kingfisher offers delicious Malaysian food and seafood on hearty dinner buffets, with live cooking stations serving to enhance guests' dining experience.

For more intimate fine dining, visit Olives. As the name suggests, this is a distinctly Mediterranean-themed venue, and is a mouth-watering source of French, Spanish, Italian and Greek cuisine. For impromptu get-togethers or casual evenings, guests can choose to dine al fresco at the Sunset Bar and Grill, letting the friendly staff help in choosing between a succulent steak from the char grill or an authentic, made-to-order pizza as they admire the setting sun.

Traditional music is the very heart and soul of the culture of the people of Sabah, and Nexus Resort Karambunai guests can experience its unique sounds first-hand with regular dances and performances held in the shaded gardens. As the evenings get later and livelier, take it up a notch at the Horizon Lounge or at the Darlin' Darlin' Fun Pub.

Seclusion and five-star luxury, beautifully framed by an unsurpassed natural backdrop—this is what the breathtaking Nexus Resort Karambunai is all about.

rooms
485

food
Noble House: Sze Chuan and Cantonese • Olives: Mediterranean • Sunset Bar and Grill: barbecue • Penyu: international • The Kingfisher: Malaysian

drink
Golfers' Lounge • The Horizon Lounge • Darlin' Darlin' Fun Pub • Splashes

features
high-speed Internet access • gym • jacuzzi • pools • tennis courts • squash court • water sports • golf course • Nexie Club • Lagoon Park • Nature Park

nearby
local markets • Kiulu white water rafting • Kinabalu Park

contact
Off Jalan Sepangar Bay, Locked Bag 100 88993 Kota Kinabalu, Sabah • telephone: +60.88.411 222 • facsimile: +60.88.411 020 • email: info@nexusresort.com • website: www.nexusresort.com

the kudat riviera

When tourism visionary Phil Dobson first came up with the idea of acquiring some of Borneo's most unspoilt coastline to create an idyllic and diverse eco-luxury villa resort through his company Exquisite Borneo Villas (EBV), he was unprepared for the response. No longer drawn to the overcrowding and overexploitation of Phuket and Bali, he found that people were genuinely looking for something a little more private and out of the way, yet easily accessible and closer to nature.

After years of combing the shores of Southeast Asia to find the ideal location, Dobson found it on the Kudat Peninsula, in Sabah. The Kudat Riviera, as it is now known, is the ultimate escape from the stresses of urban life, and coastal destinations do not come better than this. Nestled at the tip of northern Borneo, the Kudat Riviera's green hills, coconut groves and rice paddies roll down to mile upon mile of deserted white sandy beaches, bays and private coves, lapped by crystalline, emerald waters exploding with marine life. And with Dobson's eco-friendly development plan, this is exactly how the place will remain, for the exclusive enjoyment of its inhabitants.

With the full backing of the Malaysian government and Sabah's tourist board, Dobson has made the preservation of this rare, natural wonderland paramount. Instead of hundreds of villas crammed on to every square inch of beachfront, Dobson opted for a super low-density resort, so that with a total of 30 hectares (75 acres) of land, there will only be 33 luxury villa estates, with plot sizes ranging from ⅕ hectare (½ acre) to 2 hectares (5 acres) each. In this manner, the Kudat Riviera can be experienced and conserved for generations to come.

Furthermore, before embarking on the project, an intensive full environmental impact and livelihood integration study was carried out as a means to identify ways to enhance local industries and the well-being of the local Rungus community. In short, Dobson wanted to be completely satisfied that none of the elements involved in the creation of the Kudat Riviera stood to lose

out, be it the indigenous flora and fauna, the coral reefs, the inhabitants of the community or the ecosystems.

As it is, investors can rest assured that the resort is ecologically sound. Indeed, the Kudat Riviera is staying true to its philosophy of achieving oneness with nature by embracing 'green' practices and using all-natural and sustainable materials.

As for potential natural disasters, with tsunamis hitting the headlines in recent years, many would be forgiven for thinking that the Kudat Riviera would be subject to these devastating seismic phenomena that have wrought havoc in much of Southeast Asia. But this is not the case; scientific research has proven that because of its geographical position, the west coast of

Kudat Karma—stretching along 10 km (6 miles) of pristine coastline. Needless to say, the properties are built with natural materials throughout, to blend seamlessly into the landscape. Walls and swimming pools are constructed with natural Jogya and Ceribon stone, while tropical water hyacinth and bamboo furnishings harmonise with the handcrafted alang-alang thatched grass roofs, giving an authentic Asian finish to the rustic elegance of the interiors.

And sumptuously elegant they are, as exemplified by the Rice Barn Villas, already highly sought-after for rental and built in the style of a traditional Sulawesi rice barn. With two to three delectable bedrooms, and a natural stone infinity-edge pool, these charming villas provide but a taste of the extraordinary lengths that EBV will go to in order to create one of the world's most exclusive resorts.

Standing a stone's throw away from the beach and commanding breathtaking views from the upper-floor balconies and open living areas, Rice Barn Villas are nothing short of dream villas. Balinese-style spa bathrooms, with carved stone tubs, exotic showers and an adjoining, private open-air garden all make for a unique bathing experience. The kitchen is equipped to satisfy the needs of even the most professional of chefs, while thatched barbecue and beach gazebos permit maximum enjoyment of the great outdoors. That is to say nothing of the al fresco gym

Sabah is protected from any such tectonic activity. Moreover, it has for many years been known as 'the land beneath the wind' because it stands outside the typhoon belt, freeing it from the typhoon force winds and driving rain that hit Hong Kong and other areas of Southeast Asia, making Sabah—and consequently, the Kudat Riviera—a unique and standout vacation spot.

With three different styles of exquisitely appointed villas to choose from and glorious locations on the beach front, perched upon cliff tops or nestled on hillsides, decision making will not be easy. The 33 properties are divided into two unique areas, incorporating beach, private cove and hill villas (aptly known as Sky Villas)—The Coconut Reef Club and facility, where fitness fanatics can work out to the sound of humming crickets and feel the fresh sea breeze against their skin.

Every detail has been carefully thought of for the convenience of all guests. A state-of-the-art audiovisual system, complete with an LCD TV, DVD player and surround sound, makes for an ideal in-house cinema, and the laptop with Internet access keeps those far from home in touch. No need to worry about getting around in the midday heat either, since an electric buggy is on hand to take care of that.

The stunning Pandanas Villas also come equipped to six-star standards and are a pleasure to behold. Here, the innovative

THIS PAGE: *A Coco Villa set on a lush, 1-hectare (2.5-acre) private estate.*
OPPOSITE (FROM TOP): *Guests will find a tropical idyll at the Kudat Riviera; experience ultimate relaxation at any of the well-appointed villas.*

THIS PAGE: An ideal spot for a quick afternoon nap, an intimate chat or a cosy read.

OPPOSITE (FROM LEFT): The abundant use of natural materials in the villas is sure to please even the most environmentally conscious of holidaymakers; soak away the stresses of the day at the spa-style bathroom.

construction plan involves two A-frame buildings connected by a bridge crossing over an infinity-edge pool. The magnificent 279-sq-m (3,000-sq-ft) residence allows for spacious open-air ground floor reception rooms and three bedrooms, each adjoined by spa bathrooms. The bedrooms upstairs open out onto expansive balconies with views over lush gardens, gazebos and out to sea.

The extraordinary Coco Villas offer a staggering 557-sq-m (6,000-sq-ft) of living space, including four oversized bedrooms. The high-beamed roofs create a feeling of cool, tropical grandeur and with a 139-sq-m (1500-sq-ft) natural stone infinity-edge pool embracing the entire front of the villa, a truly

open-air ambience is created. Ingeniously concealed amid the fragrant coconut and merbau timber of the interiors are high-tech gadgets that will make even the most cosmopolitan feel at home.

And just as EBV has anticipated its guests' every need within the heavenly villas, once the entire development is complete, several gourmet restaurants and a spa resort will also grace the peninsula to make living at the Kudat Riviera living much more enjoyable.

It is hardly surprising to find out that all 33 villas have quickly sold out, considering that the Kudat Riviera won awards for Best Architecture and Best Development in the International Property Awards. Not only that, *Asia Pacific Tropical Homes* gave the Kudat Riviera the Top of the Region Award for the Finest Development in the Asia Pacific Region.

Swimming in the clear waters of the Kudat Riviera with not a care in the world, one feels as far away from civilisation as is humanly possible. However, getting there is remarkably straightforward. Sabah's capital, Kota Kinabalu, can be reached on multiple daily flights from Kuala Lumpur, Singapore and Hong Kong. From there, a chartered helicopter or scheduled MAS Wings flight will have the fortunate few in Kudat within 40 minutes, or in just two and a half hours by car.

It is not just the dreamlike beaches and other-worldly peacefulness that has people talking about the Kudat Riviera, for Sabah offers a wide array of sporting and ecological activities to suit every taste. Calm, warm seas offer the ideal conditions for water sports such as sailing and windsurfing, and exceptional scuba diving and snorkelling on some of the world's finest reefs. Spectacular water-side golf courses abound as do opportunities for cycling or quad-biking on jungle trails. Hard-core hikers could take a climb up the monumental Mount Kinabalu, the highest peak in Southeast Asia, and enjoy awe-inspiring, panoramic views.

Those with a more adventurous spirit might try paragliding over the picturesque coastal plains, or white-water rafting on the Kiulu River. Wildlife enthusiasts, on the other hand, will love the Sepilok Orangutan Rehabilitation Centre, a visit to the Turtle Islands or trekking in the Maliau Basin, one of the world's few remaining primal virgin forests. Courtesy of Touchdown Helicopter and Luxury Yacht Charters—another of Dobson's multiple Sabah-based enterprises—visitors to the region can also experience its rare beauty from the sea and from the skies.

Thee are few places left on earth where nature's timeless beauty has been left untouched and virtually undiscovered since its creation, and Sabah is one of them. A visit, or better still, an extended stay on the Kudat Riviera is destined to be an experience not easily forgotten and the perfect spot from which to enjoy the natural diversity of Sabah.

rooms
33 villas

food
@mosphere Rustique • @mosphere Nautique • Caviar Sky Lounge: Western, Asian and Pacific Rim

drink
bars and lounges

features
pools • spa • spa dining

nearby
Tip of Borneo • Turtle Island Park • Sepilok Orangutan Rehabilitation Centre • Mantanani Island • Sukau Rainforest Lodge

contact
telephone: +60.88.249 276 •
facsimile: +60.88.256 408 •
email: info@exquisiteborneovillas.com •
website: www.exquisiteborneovillas.com

@mosphere modern dining

Kota Kinabalu, the capital of Sabah in eastern Malaysia, is not the most obvious place in the world to find a 32-floor masterpiece of modern architecture, but then this is just an example of the many surprises to be found in this balmy, tropical city. The Sabah Foundation Tower, also known as Menara Tun Mustapha, was constructed with remarkable foresight in the late 1970s, using progressive technology that permits the entire tube-like structure to suspend from a single central column, on high-tensile steel rods. And, as if this feat of engineering was not sufficiently impressive, the 18th floor rotates 360° every hour to allow panoramic views across the city, the Crocker Mountains and out over the islands of the South China Sea.

With Sabah now clearly developing as a high-end tourism destination, with its unspoilt white sand beaches, shallow water reefs rich with marine life and countless other outdoor pursuits, the only thing missing was a restaurant showcasing the region's finest cuisine. It was the Touchdown World Travel Group, operators of Touchdown Luxury Yachts and Helicopter Charters and Asia Extreme Group, that stepped in to fill the void, establishing @mosphere restaurant in 2006.

It seemed only logical that the revolving floor of the Sabah Foundation Tower—which had been in disuse for 15 years—should be the chosen venue for this venture. It was an iconic location for a restaurant that has since made its mark as the chicest

THIS PAGE: Enjoy panoramic views of the city, ocean and rainforest at @mosphere.

OPPOSITE (FROM TOP): The revolving floor provides a novel dining experience for guests; sip cocktails at the bar.

seats
200

food
Pacific Rim cuisine

drink
extensive wine list

features
revolving restaurant ·
helicopter and luxury yacht service ·
state-of-the-art sound system

nearby
Kota Kinabalu · Sabah State Assembly ·
Puh Toh Si Chinese Temple· City Mosque ·
Kota Kinabalu City Bird Sanctuary

contact
18th floor, Sabah Foundation Tower
Jalan Sulaman, Kota Kinabalu, Sabah ·
telephone: +60.88.425 100 ·
email: info@atmosphererestaurant.com ·
website: www.atmosphererestaurant.com

establishment in Kota Kinabalu, serving some of the finest food, and by far the best views, in Malaysian Borneo.

The imaginative menu at @mosphere reflects influences from the Pacific Rim; the fresh ingredients are sourced locally and are crafted into tangy, delectable works of culinary art that are guaranteed to dazzle the senses. Guests might whet their appetites with some Green Lipped Mussels, prepared with ginger, lemongrass, coriander and coconut milk, before savouring the exquisite Vietnamese Laab Gai or some Malaysian specialities such as spicy satay or piquant curries. The extensive wine list provides the perfect accompaniment to these exotic flavours, while familiar desserts are given a distinctly Asian twist to round off the delectable meal.

The retro-modern interior of this unique restaurant is bedecked in vibrant oranges, greens and purples, reflecting the exuberant colours of sunset that make an evening at @mosphere so memorable. Plush sofas, veiled curtains and subtle lighting make for an elegant, yet cosy ambience meant to be enjoyed for lunch, afternoon tea, dinner or cocktails at the lively bar.

Those with a flair for adventure and a desire to experience Sabah from the sky or the sea must not miss the chance to be picked up from their hotel and taken to the restaurant by helicopter or on a luxury yacht. With a limousine service included in the package to ensure safe passage back to the hotel, guests can savour a delicious meal, relax, indulge and really enjoy the unforgettable @mosphere.

the english tea house + restaurant

THIS PAGE: Spend a lazy afternoon enjoying the cool breeze with friends and family at The English Tea House.

OPPOSITE (FROM LEFT): Wicker chairs add to the rustic charm; relish a piece of delectable cake in this intimate nook; watch the sky take on its evening hues from this spot.

There are few places on earth as exotic and shrouded in mystique as the island of Borneo. The mere mention of this unspoilt island conjures up images of mountainous, virgin rainforests teaming with fauna, along with pristine white sandy beaches bordering emerald seas, bursting with marine life. Indeed, the exceptional natural beauty of the Sabah region of East Malaysia is only enhanced by the vestiges of colonialism and nowhere is this more true than in Sandakan, formally the capital of British North Borneo.

For a true taste of 18th-century life in this remote and fascinating corner of Asia, a visit to The English Tea House & Restaurant should not be missed. Standing atop one of Sandakan's highest hills, this fine restaurant occupies a meticulously renovated colonial house, and provides sweeping views over the town and out to the bay and islands beyond. The property is adjacent to the Agnes Keith House museum—inhabited from the 1930s till 1950s by the American writer of the same name—and in true British tradition, breathtaking landscaped gardens with vast lawns, lush vegetation and even peacocks serve to frame this historical setting.

As its name suggests, this charming restaurant specialises in colonial English favourites. However, the talented chef has incorporated a tantalising selection of regional dishes into the menu, so that guests can get a taste of the best of both worlds. Only the freshest local ingredients are used to create such a delectable spread, which features old favourites such as fish and chips and shepherd's pie, alongside local delicacies like tiger prawn curry laksa or the irresistible coconut beef rendang. Given the exceptional quality of the food and the unlikely combination of cuisines, it is not surprising that the restaurant has been featured on several international cooking programmes.

No culinary establishment claiming British status would be complete without offering scones with clotted cream or traditional cakes and pastries. In this respect, The English Tea House definitely does justice to its name. The restaurant serves these treats on fine bone china, accompanied by an essential selection of teas from around the world. Of particular interest is the locally grown Sabah tea, which has been developed into flavoured varieties such as Earl Grey and English Breakfast, in cooperation with The English Tea House.

After a visit to some of the pre-eminent sights in and around Sandakan, for example the Sepilok Orangutan Rehabilitation Centre or the Labuk Bay Proboscis Monkey Sanctuary, there is no better way to spend an afternoon than a mouth-watering meal followed by a game of croquet. Guests would surely enjoy a round or two of knocking coloured balls through hoops with the use of traditional croquet mallets. For those looking to cap off a day of sightseeing in a more sedentary manner, The English Tea House's long bar offers a wide array of cocktails to soothe and refresh.

Guests keen on finding an ideal location for weddings, corporate functions and other events will not find a place more suitable than the restaurant, with its 100-seat covered terrace, air-conditioned VIP meeting and dining room for 12 and removable marquee for 100 people. Indeed, a tropical idyll is what guests will find at The English Tea House.

seats
200

food
Asian • traditional English specialities

drink
tea • cocktails

features
croquet lawn • colonial architecture • weekend barbecue • themed parties

nearby
Agnes Keith House • Rotary Observation Pavilion

contact
2002 Jalan Istana, 90000 Sandakan, Sabah • telephone: +60.89.222 544 • facsimile: +60.89.222 545 • email: info@englishteahouse.org • website: www.englishteahouse.org

touchdown luxury yacht + helicopter charters

Without a doubt it is becoming increasingly difficult to find unspoilt beach destinations; places which are relatively easy to reach, yet not built-up, polluted or generally teeming with tourists, and where natural ecosystems have not been damaged by over-exploitation. This is what distinguishes Sabah in Malaysian Borneo from the rest of the world and sets it in a league of its own.

Here, a plethora of untouched islands are inhabited only by the kaleidoscope of native species of the virgin jungles and the tropical fish and marine life that thrive on the coral reefs along their shores. These islands' powdery, white sand beaches are deserted and their emerald waters calm, shallow, warm and crystal clear. Places like these may seem like impossibly inaccessible last frontiers but

thanks to Touchdown Luxury Yacht and Helicopter Charters, reaching these islands just got a whole lot easier.

Touchdown operates a stunning fleet of motor yachts that take passengers on personalised day trips, sunset cruises or overnight getaways to experience the South China Sea in unimaginable luxury. Cruises are fully catered, with three-course gourmet meals and a highly professional crew to ensure that guests want for nothing on their exclusive retreat. Guests can meander through the isolated coves of the Tunku Abdul Rahman Marine Park, off the coast of Kota Kinabalu, or discover more remote destinations such as the Tip of Borneo or the heavenly islands of Mantanani that are virtually unreachable by other means.

THIS PAGE: *Opt for a power boat ride for a truly exciting time; spend a weekend basking in the sun on these sleek yachts.* OPPOSITE (FROM TOP): *Enjoy superb aerial views aboard Touchdown's helicopters; pristine, secluded beaches such as these are usual destinations for cruises.*

fleet
5

food
gourmet meals

drink
wine

features
sunset cruises • day charters •
2-day live aboard charters

nearby
Sabah State Museum • Sabah State Mosque

contact
Lower Level, Pacific Sutera, Sutera Harbour
Resort, 88100 Kota Kinabalu, Sabah •
telephone: +60.88.249 276 •
facsimile: +60.88.256 408

Touchdown Luxury Yacht Charters
email: kk@touchdownluxuryyachts.com •
website: www.touchdownluxuryyachts.com

Touchdown Helicopter Charters
email: kk@touchdownhelicopters.com •
website: www.touchdownhelicopters.com

For those looking for something more adventurous, a ride on the Bladerunner power boat is a must. The vessel is capable of travelling up to 70 miles (113 km) per hour, ensuring an adrenaline rush for thrill-seekers.

Touchdown is the essential option for viewing Sabah in ultimate style and its helicopter charters open up a whole realm of possibilities to experience areas literally untouched by man. Visitors are invited to fly from Kota Kinabalu airport to their resort or simply take a pleasure trip over Sabah's islands and jewelled coast. Fly through the Kiulu river valley, and land at a scenic spot to enjoy champagne and a cooling dip in the river. Heli-golfing tours, on the other hand, will take golfers to numerous world-class courses in stunning, lush water-side locations, quite unlike any other golfing trip. Perhaps the most extraordinary option, however, would be a flight around the majestic Mount Kinabalu, Southeast Asia's highest peak. Sweep down over the Maliau Basin, deep in the region's interior, to witness some of the earth's last primal, virgin forests, brimming with wildlife. A day's excursion can include a two-hour jungle trek, lunch and a refreshing swim in the picturesque Maliau waterfalls.

Surely any trip to Malaysian Borneo would be captivating but through Touchdown Yacht and Helicopter Charters, the experience will be absolutely unforgettable.

index

picturecredits+acknowledgements

The publisher would like to thank the following for permission to reproduce their photographs:

@mosphere Modern Dining front flap (middle), 47 (top), 180–181

7atenine 94–95

Adrian Kisai 30 (top left + top right), 31 (bottom + top)

AFP/Getty Images 16 (top), 28, 39 (bottom), 52, 163

Ahmad Yusni/epa/Corbis 128 (top)

Alexander Hassenstein/Getty Images 33 (top)

Alexis at The Gardens 43 (top left), 96–97

Alexis Bistro & Wine Bar at Bangsar Shopping Centre 98–99

Amanda Koster Productions/Getty Images 54 (middle)

Andrea Pistolesi/Getty Images 55

Andreas Strauss/Getty Images 57 (bottom)

Asian Heritage Row 100–101

Avillion Port Dickson 132–133

Basil Leaf Restaurant 102–103

Bon Ton Restaurant and Resort 45 (top left), 134–135

BritishIndia 112–113

Cameron Highlands Resort 63, 136–137

Carcosa Seri Negara 42, 78–79

Casa del Mar front cover (bottom right), 138–139

Cheong Fatt Tze Mansion 140–141

Dallas and John Heaton/Corbis 127 (left)

David Olsen/Getty Images back cover (bottom left), 13 (top)

Demetrio Carrasco/JAI/Corbis 71 (top)

Dimitri Vervitsiotis/Getty Images 53 (bottom)

Eastern & Oriental Hotel 142–143

EEST 44 (top)

Emetrio Carrasco/JAI/Corbis 36

Feast & Chime Restaurant, Sheraton Langkawi Beach Resort 35 (top)

Ferdinand's at The Magellan Sutera 47 (bottom)

Fletcher & Baylis/Photolibrary 160

Four Seasons Resort Langkawi back flap (top), back cover (top left), front cover (top left + top right + bottom left + bowl of spa ingredients), 46, 58 (top), 62, 128 (bottom), 144–145

Frank Seifert/Getty Images back cover (wayang kulit), 40 (top right)

Frans Lanting/Corbis 12

George Doyle/Getty Images 64

Getty Images 48, 49 (bottom left), 54 (top)

Glen Allison/Getty Images 61 (top)

Greg Elms/Getty Images 13 (bottom), 37 (bottom)

Heinrich van den Berg 58 (bottom left)

Hotel Maya 80–81

Hugh Sitton/Getty Images back cover (traditional kite), 40 (bottom)

Ian Shive/Getty Images 14, 122, 130–131

Indulgence Restaurant & Living 158–159

Islamic Arts Museum Malaysia 50 (bottom)

James Gritz/Getty Images 125

JapaMala Resorts 146–147

Jörg Sundermann 10–11

Justin Guariglia/National Geographic/Getty Images 15 (bottom)

JW Marriot Hotel Kuala Lumpur 82–83

Kazuhiro Tanda/Getty Images 53 (top)

KL Performing Arts Centre 50 (top)

Kraftangan Malaysia 54 (bottom left)

Louise Murray/Foto Natura/Getty Images 41 (bottom)

Macduff Everton/Getty Images 66–67

Mandarin Oriental, Kuala Lumpur 84–85

Marc Volk/Getty Images 57 (top left)

Martin Puddy/Getty Images 15 (top), 31 (middle), 40 (top left)

Martin Stolworthy/Getty Images 68

MATTHEW SCUBAZOO/Photolibrary 6

Michel Gotin/Getty Images 127 (right)

Mike Simons/Getty Images 59 (top)

National Art Gallery Malaysia 29 (top), 30 (middle)

National Geographic/Getty Images back cover (bird), 165 (right)

Nerovivo 104–105

Nexus Resort Karambunai 170–173

Norbert Wu/Getty Images 166, 167

Old China Café 45 (top right)

Ombak Asia 114–115

OTHK/Getty Images 76–77

Owen Franken/Corbis 16 (bottom)

Pangkor Laut Resort back cover (top right), 148–149

Panoramic Images/Getty Images 72–73

Peter Lilja/Getty Images 56

Photolibrary 26

Poppy Collection front flap (top), 106–107

Purser's Choice 116–117

Putrajaya Marriot Hotel 86–87

Ravi John 20, 21, 22, 24, 25, 27, 74 (bottom), 75, 126, 129

Robbie Shone/Getty Images 61 (bottom), 165 (left)

Robert Francis/Getty Images 60 (top)

Robert Harding/Getty Images 18–19

Royal Selangor front cover (jewellery), 49 (bottom right), 118–119

Sao Nam 43 (top right)

Sarawak Tourism front cover (rafflesia)

Schlegelmilch/Corbis 17

See Kok Shan/Picture Library 59 (bottom)

Shamshahrin Shamsudin/epa/Corbis 74 (top)

Simon Jarratt/Corbis 54 (bottom right)

SOULed OUT Kuala Lumpur 108–109

Steve Raymer/Getty Images 37 (top)

Steve Winter/Getty Images 58 (bottom right)

Sunway Resort Hotel & Spa front cover (floral bath), 2, 92–93, 88–89

Tamarind Springs back flap (bottom), 44 (bottom), 110–111

Tan Lian Hock/Picture Library 29 (bottom), 30 (bottom), 38, 39 (top)

Tanjong Jara Resort 4, 150–153

Tengku Bahar/AFP/Getty Images 33 (bottom), 71 (bottom)

The Andaman Langkawi back cover (traditional musical instruments), 45 (bottom), 51 (bottom), 154–155

The Carat Club, Kuala Lumpur 120–121

The Datai Langkawi 156–157

The English Tea House & Restaurant 182–183

The Kudat Riviera front flap (bottom), 174–179

The Ritz-Carlton, Kuala Lumpur 65, 90–91

Third Floor 43 (bottom)

Timothy Laman/Getty Images 41 (top), 57 (top right), 60 (bottom left + bottom right), 164, 168–169

Tim Pannell/Corbis 49 (middle right)

Touchdown Luxury Yacht and Helicopter Charters 184–185

Tourism Malaysia back cover (bottom right), 23

Traders Hotel 34

Wei-Ling Gallery 51 (top)

Zouk 32, 35 (bottom left + bottom right)

All other images belong to Editions Didier Millet.

directory

HOTELS AND RESORTS

Avillion Port Dickson (page 132)
3rd Mile, Jalan Pantai
71000 Port Dickson
Negeri Sembilan
telephone : +60.6.647 6688
facsimile : +60.6.647 7688
res@avillion.com
www.avillion.com

Bon Ton Restaurant + Resort (page 134)
Pantai Cenang
07000 Langkawi, Kedah
telephone : +60.4.955 3643
facsimile : +60.4.955 4791
info@bontonresort.com.my
www.bontonresort.com.my

Cameron Highlands Resort (page 136)
39000 Tanah Rata
Cameron Highlands, Pahang
telephone : +60.5.491 1100
facsimile : +60.5.491 1800
travelcentre@ytlhotels.com.my
www.cameronhighlandsresort.com

Carcosa Seri Negara (page 78)
Taman Tasik Perdana
Persiaran Mahameru
50480 Kuala Lumpur
telephone : +60.3.2295 0888
facsimile : +60.3.2282 7888
carcosa@ghmhotels.com
www.ghmhotels.com

Casa del Mar (page 138)
Jalan Pantai Cenang
07000 Mukim Kedawang
Langkawi, Kedah
telephone : +60.4.955 2388
facsimile : +60.4.955 2228
info@casadelmar-langkawi.com
www.casadelmar-langkawi.com

Cheong Fatt Tze Mansion (page 140)
14 Leith Street
10200 George Town
Penang
telephone : +60.4.262 0006
facsimile : +60.4.262 5289
cftm@tm.net.my
www.cheongfatttzemansion.com

Eastern + Oriental Hotel (page 142)
10 Lebuh Farquhar
10200 Penang
telephone : +60.4.222 2000
facsimile : +60.4.261 6333
hotel-info@e-o-hotel.com
www.e-o-hotel.com

Four Seasons Resort Langkawi (page 144)
Jalan Tanjung Rhu
07000 Langkawi, Kedah
telephone : +60.4.950 8888
facsimile : +60.4.950 8899
reservations.lan@fourseasons.com
www.fourseasons.com/langkawi

Hotel Maya (page 80)
138 Jalan Ampang
50450 Kuala Lumpur
telephone : +60.3.2711 8866
facsimile : +60.3.2711 9966
info@hotelmaya.com.my
www.hotelmaya.com.my

JapaMala Resorts (page 146)
Kampung Lanting
86000 Pulau Tioman, Pahang
telephone : +60.9.419 7777
facsimile : +60.9.419 7979
info@japamalaresorts.com
www.japamalaresorts.com

JW Marriott Hotel Kuala Lumpur (page 82)
183 Jalan Bukit Bintang
55100 Kuala Lumpur
telephone : +60.3.2715 9000
facsimile : +60.3.2715 7000
jwmh@po.jaring.my
wwwytlhotels.com.my/properties/jwmarriot

Mandarin Oriental, Kuala Lumpur (page 84)
Kuala Lumpur City Centre
PO Box 10905
50088 Kuala Lumpur
telephone : +60.3.2380 8888
facsimile : +60.3.2380 8833
mokul-sales@mohg.com
www.mandarinoriental.com

Nexus Resort Karambunai
(page 170)
Off Jalan Sepangar Bay
Locked Bag 100
88993 Kota Kinabalu, Sabah
telephone : +60.88.411 222
facsimile : +60.88.411 020
info@nexusresort.com
www.nexusresort.com

Pangkor Laut Resort (page 148)
Pangkor Laut Island
32200 Lumut, Perak
telephone : +60.5.699 1100
facsimile : +60.5.699 1200
travelcentre@ytlhotels.com
www.pangkorlautresort.com

Putrajaya Marriott Hotel
(page 86)
Putrajaya Marriott Hotel IOI Resort
62502 Putrajaya
telephone : +60.3.8949 8888
facsimile : +60.3.8949 8999
sales.hotel@marriottputrajaya.com
www.marriott.com/kulpg

Sunway Resort Hotel + Spa
(page 88)
Persiaran Lagoon, Bandar Sunway
46150 Petaling Jaya, Selangor
telephone : +60.3.7492 8000
facsimile : +60.3.7492 8001
enquirysrhs@sunwayhotels.com
www.sunwayhotels.com

Tanjong Jara Resort (page 150)
Batu 8, off Jalan Dungun
23000 Dungun, Terengganu
telephone : +60.9.845 1100
facsimile : +60.9.845 1200
tjara@ytlhotels.com
www.tanjongjararesort.com

The Andaman Langkawi
(page 154)
Jalan Teluk Datai, PO Box 94
07000 Langkawi, Kedah
telephone : +60.4.959.1088
facsimile : +60.4.959.1168
andaman@ghmhotels.com
www.theandaman.com

The Datai Langkawi (page 156)
Jalan Teluk Datai
07000 Langkawi, Kedah
telephone : +60.4.959 2500
facsimile : +60.4.959 2600
datai@ghmhotels.com
www.langkawi-resorts.com/datailk

The Kudat Riviera (page 174)
telephone : +60.88.249 276
facsimile : +60.88.256 408
info@exquisiteborneovillas.com
www.exquisiteborneovillas.com

The Ritz-Carlton, Kuala Lumpur
(page 90)
168 Jalan Imbi
55100 Kuala Lumpur
telephone : +60.3.2142 8000
facsimile : +60.3.2143 8080
ritzkl@ritzcarlton.com.my
www.ritzcarlton.com

**The Villas at Sunway Resort
Hotel + Spa** (page 92)
Persiaran Lagoon, Bandar Sunway
46150 Petaling Jaya, Selangor
telephone : +60.3.7495 1646
facsimile : +60.3.7492 8007
thevillas@sunwayhotels.com
www.sunwayhotels.com

RESTAURANTS

7atenine (page 94)
Ascott Kuala Lumpur
9 Jalan Pinang
50450 Kuala Lumpur
telephone : +60.3.2161 7789
facsimile : +60.3.2163 7789
ask@sevenatenine.com
www.sevenatenine.com

@mosphere Modern Dining
(page 180)
18th Floor, Sabah Foundation Tower
Jalan Sulaman
Kota Kinabalu, Sabah
telephone : +60.88.425 100
info@atmosphererestaurant.com
www.atmosphererestaurant.com

Asian Heritage Row (page 100)
11–01 Heritage House
33 Jalan Yap Ah Shak
50300 Kuala Lumpur
telephone : +60.3.2694 6460 or
+60.3.2694 6462
facsimile : +60.3.2694 6682
enquiry@asianheritagerow.com
www.asianheritagerow.com

Alexis @ The Gardens (page 96)
Lot F2009, 1st Floor, The Gardens
Mid Valley City, Lingkaran Syed Putra
59200 Kuala Lumpur
telephone : +60.3.2287 2281
info@alexis.com.my
www.alexis.com.my

**Alexis Bistro + Wine Bar at
Bangsar Shopping Centre**
(page 98)
Lot F15A, 1st Floor
Bangsar Shopping Centre
285 Jalan Maarof, Bukit Bandar Raya
59000 Kuala Lumpur
telephone : +60.3.2287 1388
info@alexis.com.my
www.alexis.com.my

Basil Leaf Restaurant (page 102)
35 Jalan Damai, off Jalan Tun Razak
55000 Kuala Lumpur
telephone : +60.3.2166 1689
facsimile : +60.3.2143 2689
reservation@basilleafrestaurants.com
www.basilleafrestaurants.com

Indulgence Restaurant + Living
(page 158)
14 Jalan Raja Dihilir
30350 Ipoh, Perak
telephone : +60.5.255 7051
facsimile : +60.5.242 6297
indulge@indulgencerestaurant.com
www.indulgencerestaurant.com

Nerovivo (page 104)
3A Jalan Ceylon
50200 Kuala Lumpur
telephone : +60.3.2070 3120
facsimile : +60.3.2070 3100
info@nerovivo.com
www.nerovivo.com

Poppy Collection (page 106)
8-1 Jalan P Ramlee
50250 Kuala Lumpur
telephone :+60.3.2141 8888
facsimile : +60.3.2148 1282
info@poppy-collection.com
www.poppy-collection.com

SOULed OUT Kuala Lumpur
(page 108)
20 Jalan 30/70A
Desa Sri Hartamas
50480 Kuala Lumpur
telephone : +60.3.2300 1955
facsimile : +60.3.2300 1989
yum_yum@souledout.com.my
www.souledout.com.my

Tamarind Springs (page 110)
Jalan 1, Taman TAR
Ampang, 68000 Selangor
telephone : +60.3.4256 9300
facsimile : +60.3.4251 9100
info@tamarindrestaurants.com
www.tamarindrestaurants.com

**The English Tea House +
Restaurant** (page 182)
2002 Jalan Istana
90000 Sandakan, Sabah
telephone : +60.89.222 544
facsimile : +60.89.222 545
info@englishteahouse.org
www.englishteahouse.org

SHOPS

BritishIndia (page 112)
G305A, 1 Utama Shopping Centre
Lebuh Bandar Utama
47800 Petaling Jaya
telephone : +60.3.7724 1822

Ground Floor, Great Eastern Mall
303 Jalan Ampang
50450 Kuala Lumpur
telephone : +60.3.4253 5266

Lot 111A and B, 1st Floor, Suria KLCC
Kuala Lumpur City Centre
50088 Kuala Lumpur
telephone : +60.3.2166 2282
customerservice@bi.com.my

Ombak Asia (page 114)
Lot 301-A, 3rd Floor, Suria KLCC
Kuala Lumpur City Centre
50088 Kuala Lumpur
telephone : +60.3.2161 9600
facsimile : +60.3.2161 9613
ombakklcc@hotmail.com
www.ombak.com.my

Purser's Choice (page 116)
Bangsar Village II, 2nd Floor,
Units 1b and 2
2 Jalan Telawi Satu
59100 Kuala Lumpur
telephone : +60.3.2282 1928
facsimile : +60.3.2282 1923
info@purserschoice.com
www.purserschoice.com

Royal Selangor (page 118)
4 Jalan Usahawan 6
Setapak Jaya
53300 Kuala Lumpur
telephone : +60.3.4145 6122
facsimile : +60.3.4022 3000
visitorcentre@royalselangor.com.my
www.visitorcentre.royalselangor.com

The Carat Club, Kuala Lumpur
(page 120)
Boutique
119 Jalan Maarof
Taman Bangsar
59000 Kuala Lumpur
telephone : +60.3.2284 8618
facsimile : +60.3.2284 866
bsr@thecaratclub.com

Head office:
99L Jalan Tandok, off Jalan Maarof
59000 Kuala Lumpur
telephone : +60.3.2284 8620
facsimile : +60.3.2284 8662
www.thecaratclub.com

CRUISES

**Touchdown Luxury Yacht +
Helicopter Charters** (page 184)
Lower Level, Pacific Sutera
Sutera Harbour Resort
88100 Kota Kinabalu, Sabah
telephone : +60.88.249 276
facsimile : +60.88.256 408

**Touchdown Luxury Yacht
Charters**
kk@touchdownluxuryyachts.com
www.touchdownluxuryyachts.com

Touchdown Helicopter Charters
kk@touchdownhelicopters.com
www.touchdownhelicopters.com

ARCHITECTURE

67 Tempinis
67 Jalan Tempinis Satu
Lucky Garden Bangsar
59100 Kuala Lumpur

Boh Visitor Centre
Jalan Gunung Brinchang
Brinchang, Cameron Highlands
telephone : +60.5.496 2096
info@boh.com.my
www.boh.com.my

Central Market
Lot 3.01 + 3.07, 1st Floor,
Central Market Annexe
Jalan Hang Kasturi
50050 Kuala Lumpur
telephone : +60.3.2031 0339
facsimile : +60.3.2032 2399
cm1888@streamyx.com
www.centralmarket.com.my

Cheng Hoon Teng
25 Jalan To'kong, 75200 Melaka
telephone : +60.6.282 9343
facsimile : +60.6.286 1889
info@chenghoonteng.org.my
www.chenghoonteng.org.my

Chin Woo Stadium
Jalan Hang Jebat, Kuala Lumpur
telephone : +60.3.232 4602

City Hall
Jalan Kelab, Ipoh, Perak

Court House Complex
Main Bazaar, Jalan Tun Abang Haji
Openg, Kuching

Dayabumi Complex
Jalan Sultan Hishamuddin
50050 Kuala Lumpur

Dutch Administrative Building
Stadthuys, Town Square Jalan Kota
Melaka, Malaysia

Federal House
Jalan Sultan Hishamuddin
Kuala LumpurMalaysia

Harrisons + Crosfield
70 Jalan Ampang, Kuala Lumpur

Istana Budaya
Jalan Tun Razak
50694 Kuala Lumpur
telephone : +60.3.4026 5555
facsimile : +60.3.4025 5975
info@istanabudaya.gov.my
www.istanabudaya.gov.my

Khoo Kongsi
18 Cannon Square, 10200 Penang
telephone : +60.4.261 4609

KL Performing Arts Centre
Sentul Park, Jalan Strachan
51100 Kuala Lumpur
telephone : +60.3.4047 9010
facsimile : +60.3.4047 9011
www.klpac.com

**Kuala Lumpur International
Airport**
64000 KLIA, Selangor
telephone : +60.3.8776 2000
publicrelation@malaysiaairports.
com.my
www.klia.com.my

Kuala Lumpur Railway Station
Jalan Sultan Hishamuddin
Kuala Lumpur
telephone : +60.3.2274 6063

Kuala Lumpur Tower
2 Jalan Punchak, off Jalan P Ramlee
50250 Kuala Lumpur
telephone : +60.3.2020 5444
facsimile : +60.3.2098 7001
menara@manarakl.com.my
www.menarakl.com.my

**Larut Matang + Selama
District Office**
Taiping, Perak

Loke Mansion
273A Jalan Medan Tuanku
50300 Kuala Lumpur

Loke Yew Building
4 Jalan Mahkamah Persekutuan
50050 Kuala Lumpur

**Malayan Railway Administration
Building**
Jalan Sultan Hishamuddin
Kuala Lumpur
telephone : +60.3.2274 6063

Masjid Jamek
Jalan Tun Perak
50400 Kuala Lumpur
telephone : +60.3.2693 6661

Masjid Kampung Laut
Nilam Puri
Kota Bharu, Kelantan

Masjid Kapitan Keling
Masjid Kapitan Keling Road
10200 Penang

Masjid Tengkera
Jalan Tengkera, Melaka

Masjid Ubudiah
Bukit Chandan
Kuala Kangsar, Malaysia

Masjid Zahir
Jalan Pekan Melayu, Alor Star, Kedah

Menara Maybank
100 Jalan Tun Perak
50050 Kuala Lumpur

Menara Mesiniaga
SS (Section) 16 Subang Jaya
46350 Selangor, Malaysia

Menara TM
Jalan Pantai Bahru, Kuala Lumpur
www.tm.com.my

directory

National Library of Malaysia
(Perpustakaan Negara Malaysia)
232 Tun Razak, 50572 Kuala Lumpur

National Museum (Muzium Negara Malaysia)
Jalan Damansara
50566 Kuala Lumpur
telephone : +60.3.2282 6255
facsimile : +60.3.2282 6434
info@museum.gov.my
www.museum.gov.my

National Mosque
Jalan Sultan Hishamuddin
Kuala Lumpur, Malaysia
telephone : +60.3.2693 7905
facsimile : +60.3.2913 696

Odeon Cinema
Jalan Tuanku Abdul Rahman
Kuala Lumpur

Oriental Building
Jalan Tun Perak/Jalan Melaka

Panggung Bandaraya
Sultan Abdul Samad Building
Jalan Raja, Kuala Lumpur
telephone : +60.3.2617 6307
facsimile : +60.3.2698 3820
mfauzi@dbkl.gov.my
www.dbkl.gov.my/panggung/

Parliament House
Jalan Parlimen
50480 Kuala Lumpur

Penang Heritage Trust Office
26A Stewart Lane, 10200 Penang
telephone : +60.4.264 2631
phtrust@po.jaring.my
www.pht.org.my

Perak Museum
Jalan Taming Sari
34000 Taiping, Perak
telephone : +60.5.807 2057
facsimile : +60.5.806 3643

Petronas Twin Towers
Kuala Lumpur City Centre
50088 Kuala Lumpur
skybridge@petronas.com.my
www.petronastwintowers.com.my

Royal Selangor Club
The Padang
telephone : +60.3.2692 7166
general@rscweb.org.my
rscweb.org.my

Rubber Research Institute of Malaya
260 Jalan Ampang
50450 Kuala Lumpur

Rudinara
Sungei Merab, Bangi Selangor

Safari Roof House
463 Jalan 17/13A
Petaling Jaya, Selangor

Sarawak Museum
Jalan Tun Abang Haji Openg
93566 Kuching
telephone : +60.82.244 232
facsimile : +60.82.246 680
museum@po.jaring.my
www.museum.sarawak.gov.my

Sekeping Serendah
67 Jalan Tempinis Satu
Lucky Garden, Bangsar
59100 Kuala Lumpur
telephone : +60.12.324 6552
mail@serendah.com
www.serendah.com

Sinurambi
88812 Kota Kinabalu, Sabah
telephone : +60.88.228 296
facsimile : +60.88.474 944
mills@borneocountrystay.com
www.borneocountrystay.com

State Assembly Buildings
Light Street, Penang 10200

St Paul's Church
Bukit St Paul, 75000 Melaka

St Peter's Church
Jalan Bendahara, 75100 Melaka

Sultan Abdul Samad Building
Jalan Raja, 50050 Kuala Lumpur
telephone : +60.3.2696 6135

Tabung Haji
Jalan Tun Razak

Town Hall
Jalan Padang Kota Lama
10200 Penang

Universiti Teknologi Petronas
Bandar Seri Iskandar
31750 Tronoh, Perak, Malaysia
telephone : +60.5.368 8000
facsimile : +60.5.365 4075
aslinda_j@petronas.com.my
www.utp.edu.my

Wei-Ling Gallery
8 Jalan Scott, Brickfields
50470 Kuala Lumpur, Malaysia
telephone : +60.3.2260 1106
facsimile : +60.3.2260 1107
weiling@weiling-gallery.com
weiling-gallery.com

Wisma Ekran
16 Jalan Tangsi
50480 Kuala Lumpur

VISUAL ARTS + CRAFTS

Gerai OA
telephone: +60.19.751 8686
szening@gmail.com
www.coac.org.my

Kim Fashion
170–4–77 Gurney Plaza
10250 Penang
telephone : +60.4.226 6110

33 Jalan Cantonment, 10250 Penang
telephone : +60.4.227 0900
facsimile : +60.4.229 3643

Pura Tanjung Sabtu
5728 Kampung Tanjung Sabtu
Mukim Manir
21200 Kuala Terengganu
Terengganu, Malaysia
telephone : +60.9.615 3655
facsimile : +60.9.615 5013
www.puratanjungsabtu.com

Pulau Keladi
Perniagaan Sutera Pulau Keladi
Bangunan Karyaneka, Kampung
Budaya Pulau Keladi
Pekan, Pahang

Rimbun Dahan
Km 27 Jalan Kuang, Kuang
48050 Selangor
telephone : +60.3.6038 3690 or
+60.3.6038 1417
www.rimbundahan.org

Tai Kheng
180–B Jalan Air Itam, Penang

Valentine Willie Fine Art
17 Jalan Telawi Tiga, 1st Floor
Bangsar Baru, 59100 Kuala Lumpur
telephone : +60.3.2284 2348
facsimile : +60.3.2282 5190
info@vwfa.net
www.vwfa.net

BARS, CLUBS + CAFÉS

32 @ The Mansion
32 Jalan Sultan Ahmad Shah
10050 Penang
telephone : +60.4.262 2232

Attic
61–2 Jalan Bangkung
Bukit Bandaraya, Bangsar
59100 Kuala Lumpur
telephone : +60.3.2093 8842
info@attickl.com
www.attickl.com

Bagan Bar + Restaurant
18 Jalan Bagan Jermal
10250 Penang
telephone : +60.4.226 4977

Bar SaVanh
Asian Heritage Row
62–64 Jalan Doraisamy
50300 Kuala Lumpur
telephone : +60.3.2697 1180
facsimile : +60.3.2697 1181
www.asianheritagerow.com

Beach Blanket Babylon
16 Lebuh Bishop
10200 George Town, Penang
telephone : +60.4.263 8101

Bing!
84 Jalan Padungan, Chinatown
93000 Kuching, Sarawak
telephone : +60.82.410 188
facsimile : +60.82.259 188

Chinoz on the Park
G47 Suria KLCC
Kuala Lumpur City Centre
50088 Kuala Lumpur
telephone : +60.3.2166 8277
www.suriaklcc.com.my

Cynna House Lounge
Asian Heritage Row
28–40 Jalan Doraisamy
50350 Kuala Lumpur
telephone : +60.3.2694 2888
facsimile : +60.3.2692 5668
unwired@theloftkl.com
www.theloftkl.com

Frangipani Restaurant + Bar
25 Changkat Bukit Bintang
50200 Kuala Lumpur
telephone : +60.3.2144 3001
facsimile : +60.3.2145 3001
www.frangipani.com.my

Glo
A8 The Garage, 2 Penang Road
10000 Penang
telephone : +60.4.261 6066
facsimile : +60.4.262 4066
party@glo.com.my
www.glo.com.my

Grappa
Jalan Padungan, Kuching

Heritage Mansion
Heritage Avenue
18–26 Jalan Kamunting
Asian Heritage Row
50300 Kuala Lumpur
telephone : +60.3.2698 8282
facsimile : +60.3.2698 8280
www.asianheritagerow.com

House + Co
Lot S15, 2nd Floor, East Wing
Bangsar Shopping Centre
285 Jalan Maarof, Bukit Bandaraya
59000 Kuala Lumpur
telephone : +60.3.2094 4393/3139
facsimile : +60.3.2094 3198
info@houseandco.com.my
www.houseandco.com.my

Indulgence Restaurant + Jazz Room
15 Lorong Cecil Rae
Taman Canning, Ipoh
telephone : +60.5.549 6941

La Bodega Deli
Ground Floor, 18 Jalan Telawi Dua
Bangsar Baru
59100 Kuala Lumpur
telephone : +60.3.2287 8318
facsimile : +60.3.2287 6318

Luna Bar
34th Floor, Menara PanGlobal
Jalan Punchak, off Jalan P Ramlee
50250 Kuala Lumpur
telephone : +60.3.2332 7777
facsimile : +60.3.2381 2085

Marketplace
4A Lorong Yap Kwan Seng
50450 Kuala Lumpur
telephone : +60.3.2166 0750

Nam Restaurant
Bon Ton Restaurant + Resort
Pantai Cenang
07000 Langkawi, Kedah
telephone : +60.4.955 6787
facsimile : +60.4.955 4791
info@bonton.com.my
www.bontonresort.com.my

No Black Tie
17 Jalan Mesui, 50200 Kuala Lumpur
Golden Triangle, Kuala Lumpur
telephone : +60.3.2142 3737
noblacktie@gmail.com

Palate Palette
21 Jalan Mesui, off Jalan Nagasari
50200 Kuala Lumpur
telephone : +60.3.2142 2148
facsimile : +60.3.2143 2148

Qba
The Westin Kuala Lumpur
199 Jalan Bukit Bintang
55100 Kuala Lumpur
telephone : +60.3.2731 8333
facsimile : +60.3.2731 8000
twkl.reservations@westin.com
www.starwoodhotels.com

Sands
Tanjung Rhu Resort Langkawi
Mukim Ayer Hangat
07000 Langkawi, Kedah
telephone : +60.4.959 1033
facsimile : +60.4.959 1899
resort@tanjungrhu.com.my
www.tanjungrhu.com.my

Senso
Hilton Kuching Hotel
Jalan Tunku Abdul Rahman
93100 Kuching, Sarawak
telephone : +60.82.248 200
facsimile : +60.82.428 984
kuching@hilton.com
www1.hilton.com

Shenanigan's Fun Pub
Hyatt Regency Kinabalu
Jalan Datuk Salleh Sulong
88991 Kota Kinabalu, Sabah
telephone : +60.88.221 234
facsimile : +60.88.218 909
reservation.hrkinabalu@hyattintl.
com
kinabalu.regency.hyatt.com

SkyBar
33rd Floor, Trader's Hotel, Kuala
Lumpur
Kuala Lumpur City Centre
50088 Kuala Lumpur
telephone : +60.3.2332 9888
facsimile : +60.3.2332 2666
thkl@shangri-la.com
www.tradershotels.com

Slippery Senoritas
Lot B3A The Garage, 2 Penang Road
10000 Penang
telephone : +60.4.263 6868
facsimile : +60.4.261 9868
feedback@slipperysenoritas.com
www.slipperysenoritas.com

Soho
64 Jalan Padungan, 93100 Kuching

Soho Beach Bar
Batu Ferringhi Road

Soho Freehouse
50 Penang Road, 10000 Penang
telephone : +60.4.263 3331
sohofh@streamyx.com

Sunken Pool Bar
Berjaya Langkawi Beach +
Spa Resort
Karung Berkunci 200, Burau Bay
07000 Langkawi, Kedah
telephone : +60.4.959 1888
facsimile : +60.4.959 1886
reservation@b-langkawi.com.my
www.berjayaresorts.com

Telawi Street Bistro
1–3 Jalan Telawi Tiga, Bangsar Baru
59100 Kuala Lumpur
telephone : +60.3.2284 3168
facsimile : +60.3.2284 6398
info@gastrodome.com.my
www.gastrodome.com.my

The Pavilion
Jalan Teluk Datai
07000 Langkawi, Kedah
telephone : +60.4.959 2500
facsimile : +60.4.959 2600
datai@ghmhotels.com
www.ghmhotels.com

The Vintry
130 Jalan Kasah, Medan Damansara
50490 Kuala Lumpur
telephone : +60.3.2094 8262
facsimile : +60.3.2094 8262
yhwong@thevintry.com.my
www.thevintry.com.my

Twenty One Kitchen + Bar
20–1 Changkat Bukit Bintang
50200 Kuala Lumpur
telephone : +60.3.2142 0021
facsimile : +60.3.2141 0121
info@twentyone.com.my

Velvet Underground
Zouk Club Malaysia
113 Jalan Ampang
50450 Kuala Lumpur
telephone : +60.3.2171 1997
facsimile : + 60.3.2171 1998
info@zoukclub.com.my
www.zoukclub.com.my

Zeta Bar
Hilton Kuala Lumpur
3 Jalan Stesen Sentral
50470 Kuala Lumpur
telephone : +60.3.2264 2264
facsimile : +60.3.2264 2266
kuala-lumpur@hilton.com
www.kl-studio.com/zetabar.html

Zouk
113 Jalan Ampang
50450 Kuala Lumpur
telephone : +60.3.2171 1997
facsimile : + 60.3.2171 1998
info@zoukclub.com.my
www.zoukclub.com.my

BEST PLACES

Alexis
29A Jalan Telawi Tiga, Bangsar Baru
59100 Kuala Lumpur
telephone : +60.3.2284 2880
www.alexis.com.my

Coliseum Café + Hotel
98–100 Jalan Tuanku Abdul
Rahman, 50100 Kuala Lumpur
telephone : +60.3.2692 6270

La Bodega
16 Jalan Telawi Dua
59100 Kuala Lumpur
telelphone: +60.3.2287 8318
facsimile : + 60.3.2287 6318

Sarawak Cultural Village
Pantai Damai, Santubong
PO Box 2632
93752 Kuching, Sarawak
telephone : +60.82.846 411
facsimile : +60.82.846 988
info@scv.com.my
www.scv.com.my

Sri Kandaswamy Temple
3 Lorong Scott, 50470 Kuala Lumpur
telephone : +60.3.2274 2987
facsimile : +60.3.2274 0288
enquiries@srikandaswamykovil.org

Temple of Fine Arts
114 Jalan Berhala, Brickfields
50470 Kuala Lumpur
telephone : +60.3.2274 3709 or
+60.3.2274 2969
tfakl@pc.jaring.my

DINING

Bijan Bar + Restaurant
3 Jalan Ceylon, 50200 Kuala Lumpur
telephone : +60.3.2031 3575
facsimile : +60.3.2031 3576
admin@bijanrestaurant.com
www.bijanrestaurant.com

Chia Heng Air Condition Restaurant
Lot 151/152, 5A Lorong Datuk Abang
Abdul Rahim
93450 Kuching, Sarawak
telephone : +60.82.335 888
facsimile : + 60.82.486 245

Coast Restaurant + Bar
Shangri-La's Rasa Ria Resort
Pantai Dalit Beach
89208 Tuaran, Sabah
telephone : +60.88.792 888
facsimile : +60.88.792 777
rrr@shangri-la.com
www.shangri-la.com

EEST
The Westin Kuala Lumpur
199 Jalan Bukit Bintang
55100 Kuala Lumpur
telephone : +60.3.2731 8333
facsimile : +60.3.2731 8000
twkl.reservations@westin.com
www.starwoodhotels.com

El Cerdo
43–45 Changkat Bukit Bintang
Kuala Lumpur
telephone : +60.3.2145 0511

Ferdinand's
Sutera Harbour Resort
1 Sutera Harbour Boulevard
88100 Kota Kinabalu, Sabah
telephone : +60.88.318 888
facsimile : +60.88.317 777
sutera@suteraharbour.com.my
www.suteraharbour.com

Feringgi Grill
Shangri-La's Rasa Sayang Resort + Spa
Batu Feringgi Beach, 11100 Penang
telephone : +60.4.888 8888
facsimile : +60.4.881 1800
rsr@shangri-la.com
www.shangri-la.com

Fisherman's Cove
LG10 Feast Village, Starhill Gallery
181 Jalan Bukit Bintang
55100 Kuala Lumpur
telephone : +60.3.2782 3848
facsimile : +60.3.2782 3818
wwwytlcommunity.com/fisher
manscove

Iketeru
Hilton Kuala Lumpur
3 Jalan Stesen Sentral
50470 Kuala Lumpur
telephone : +60.3.2264 2264
facsimile : +60.3.2264 2266
www.kl-studio.com

Lafite
Lobby, Shangri-La Hotel, Kuala Lumpur
11 Jalan Sultan Ismail
50250 Kuala Lumpur
telephone : +60.3.2074 3900
facsimile : +60.3.2070 1514
slkl@shangri-la.com
www.shangri-la.com

Old China Café
11 Jalan Balai Polis
50000 Kuala Lumpur
telephone : +60.3.2072 5915
facsimile : +60.3.2029 1897
leonardtee@oldchina.com.my
www.oldchina.com.my

Prego
The Westin Kuala Lumpur
199 Jalan Bukit Bintang
55100 Kuala Lumpur
telephone : +60.3.2731 8333
facsimile : +60.3.2731 8000
twkl.reservations@westin.com
www.starwoodhotels.com

Port View
Lot 18, Ground Floor
Anjung Samudera
Jalan Tun Fuad Stephens
88000 Kota Kinabalu, Sabah
telephone : +60.88.221 753
facsimile : +60.88.252 812
www.portview.com.my

Ristorante Beccari
Merdeka Palace Hotel + Suites
Jalan Tun Abang Haji Openg
93000 Kuching, Sarawak
telephone : +60.82.258 000
facsimile : +60.82 425 400
info@merdekapalace.com
www.merdekapalace.com

Sao Nam
25 Jalan Tingkat Tong Shin
50200 Kuala Lumpur
telephone : +60.3.2144 1225
facsimile : +60.3.2144 8225
pliao800@gmail.com
www.saonam.com.my

Steakhouse
Hilton Kuching Hotel
Jalan Tunku Abdul Rahman
93100 Kuching, Sarawak
telephone : +60.82.248 200
facsimile : +60.82.428 984
kuching@hilton.com
www1.hilton.com

The 1885
Eastern + Oriental Hotel
10 Lebuh Farquhar, 10200 Penang
telephone : +60.4.222 2000
facsimile : +60.4.261 6333
hotel-info@e-o-hotel.com
www.e-o-hotel.com

The Dining Room
Carcosa Seri Negara
Taman Tasik Perdana
Persiaran Mahameru
50480 Kuala Lumpur
telephone : +60.3.2282 1888
facsimile : +60.3.2282 6868
carcosa@ghmhotels.com
www.ghmhotels.com

The Gulai House
Jalan Teluk Datai, PO Box 94
07000 Langkawi, Kedah
telephone : +60.4.959.1088
facsimile : +60.4.959.1168
reservations@theandaman.com
www.theandaman.com

The Olive
Genting Hotel
69000 Genting Highlands, Pahang
telephone : +60.3.6101 1118
facsimile : +60.3.6101 1888
www.genting.com

The Smokehouse
PO Box 77, Tanah Rata
39007 Cameron Highlands, Pahang
telephone : +60.5.491 1215
facsimile : +60.5.491 1214
cameron@thesmokehouse.com.my
www.thesmokehouse.com.my

Third Floor
JW Marriott Hotel Kuala Lumpur
183 Jalan Bukit Bintang
55100 Kuala Lumpur
telephone : +60.3.2715 9000
facsimile : +60.3.2715 7000
www.marriott.com

FASHION + DESIGNERS

Beatrice Looi
1st Floor, Bangsar Village II
2 Jalan Telawi Satu, Bangsar Baru
59100 Kuala Lumpur
telephone : +60.3.2282 5889
www.beatricelooi.com

Bernard Chandran Flagship Boutique
2nd Floor, KL Plaza
179 Jalan Bukit Bintang
55100 Kuala Lumpur
telephone : +60.3.2145 0534
facsimile : +60.3.2145 0539
info@bernardchandran.com
www.bernardchandran.com

Eclipse
1st Floor, Suria KLCC
Kuala Lumpur City Centre
50088 Kuala Lumpur
telephone : +60.3.2382 0259

1st Floor, Lot 10 Shopping Centre
50 Jalan Sultan Ismail
50250 Kuala Lumpur
telephone : +60.3.2145 7303

1st Floor, Mid Valley Megamall
Kuala Lumpur
telephone : +60.3.2287 8278

1st Floor, 1 Utama Shopping Centre
1 Lebuh Bandar Utama
Bandar Utama City Centre
Bandar Utama
47800 Petaling Jaya, Selangor
telephone : +60.3.7726 8223

Lot G1.63, Sunway Pyramid
3 Jalan PJS 11/15, Bandar Sunway
46150 Petaling Jaya, Selangor
telephone : +60.3.5622 1931

Lot 4.15, Pavilion
168 Jalan Bukit Bintang
55100 Kuala Lumpur
telephone : +60.3.2141 9527
www.eclipse.com.my

Eric Choong
Wedding Treasures Sdn Bhd
61–1 and 63–1 Jalan Telawi Tiga
Bangsar Baru
59100 Kuala Lumpur
telephone : +60.3.2283 2113
facsimile : +60.3.2283 2117
enquiry@ericchoong.com
www.ericchoong.com

Farah Khan
Aseana
The Melium Galleria
G17-18, Ground Floor, Suria KLCC
50088 Kuala Lumpur
telephone : +60.3.2382 9988
facsimile : +60.3.2382 6888
www.farahkhan.com

Jimmy Choo
Lot G43, Ground Floor, Suria KLCC
Kuala Lumpur City Centre
Kuala Lumpur 50088
telephone : +60.3.2300 7788
www.jimmychoo.com

Key Ng
F128, 1st Floor, 1 Utama Shopping
Centre, 1 Lebuh Bandar Utama
Bandar Utama City Centre
Bandar Utama
47800 Petaling Jaya, Selangor
telephone : +60.3.7728 8939

Lot127, 1st Floor, The Curve
Mutiara Damansara
47800 Petaling Jaya, Selangor
telephone : +60.3.7727 9939

Sungei Wang Plaza (Ladies wear)
Lower Ground Floor, Sungei Wang
Plaza, Jalan Sultan Ismail
50250 Kuala Lumpur
telephone : +60.3.2144 2939

Sungei Wang Plaza (Men's wear)
F143, 1st Floor, Sungei Wang Plaza
Jalan Sultan Ismail
50250 Kuala Lumpur
telephone : +60.3.2144 4939

Avenue K (Men's wear)
Lot L1-12, 1st Floor, 156 Jalan Ampang
50450 Kuala Lumpur
www.keyng.com.my

Khoon Hooi
Unit F19B, Explore Floor
Starhill Gallery
181 Jalan Bukit Bintang
55100 Kuala Lumpur
telephone : +60.3.2142 6032

Unit S-18, 2201 Fashion Avenue @
The Gardens
Mid Valley City, Lingkaran Syed Putra
59200 Kuala Lumpur

Inspire by Khoon Hooi
Lot C, F082-F088
1st Floor, Sungei Wang Plaza
99 Jalan Bukit Bintang
55100 Kuala Lumpur
telephone : +60.3.2145 6032
www.khoonhooi.com

Malaysian International Fashion Alliance
C139 KL Plaza Court
Jalan Bukit Bintang
55100 Kuala Lumpur
telephone : +60.3.2143 3098
facsimile : +60.3.2148 3087
info@m-ifa.com
www.m-ifa.com

Melinda Looi Couture
279 Jalan Maarof
Bangsar, Bukit Bandaraya
59100 Kuala Lumpur
telephone : +60.3.2093 2279
facsimile : +60.32094 2279
info@melindalooi.com
www.melindalooi.com.my

directory

Tom Abang Saufi
Ethnicite Sdn Bhd
3rd Floor, Wisma RA
12 Jalan Dang Wangi
50100 Kuala Lumpur
telephone : +60.3.2693 1003
facsimile : +60.3.2693 3002
admin@tomsaufi.com
www.tomsaufi.com

Zang Toi Boutique
Bangsar Shopping Centre
283 Jalan Maarof, Bangsar
59100 Kuala Lumpur
telephone : +60.3.2095 1109

Great Eastern Mall, Jalan Ampang
telephone : +60.3.4252 1375

GALLERIES, MUSEUMS + THEATRES

Annexe@Central Market
Lot 3.01 and 3.07, 1st Floor
Central Market Annexe, Jalan Hang
Kasturi, 50050 Kuala Lumpur
telephone : +60.3.2031 0339
facsimile : +60.3.2032 2399
cm1888@streamyx.com
www.centralmarket-kl.com.my

Cat Museum
Ground Floor, Kuching North
City Hall, Bukit Siol
Jalan Semariang, Petra Jaya
93050 Kuching, Sarawak
telephone : +60.82.446 688
catmuseum@dbku.gov.my
www.dbku.gov.my/catmuseum.htm

Galeri PETRONAS
341–343 Ampang Mall, Suria KLCC
Kuala Lumpur City Centre
50088 Kuala Lumpur
telephone : +60.3.2051 7770
zettia@petronas.com.my
www.galeripetronas.com.my

Ibrahim Hussein Museum + Cultural Foundation
Pasir Tengkorak
07000 Langkawi, Kedah
telephone : +60.4.959 4669
facsimile : +60.4.959 4670
ibhussein@ihmcf.org
www.ihmcf.org

Instant Café Theatre
1 Jalan 10/12, Petaling Jaya
46000 Selangor
telephone : +60.3.7960 2214
info@instantcafetheatre.com
www.instantcafetheatre.com

Islamic Arts Museum Malaysia
Jalan Lembah Perdana
50480 Kuala Lumpur
telephone : +60.3.2274 2020
facsimile : +60.3.2274 0529
info@iamm.org.my
www.iamm.org.my

Malaysian Philharmonic Orchestra
Ground Floor, Tower 2
Petronas Twin Towers
50088 Kuala Lumpur
telephone : +60.3.2051 7007
facsimile : +60.3.2051 7077
www.malaysianphilharmonic.com

National Art Gallery
2 Jalan Temerloh, off Jalan Tun Razak
53200 Kuala Lumpur
telephone : +60.3.4025 4990
facsimile : +60.3.4025 4987
mnajib@artgallery.gov.my
www.artgallery.gov.my

Nelson's Gallery
Lot 84, Jalan Main Bazaar
93000 Kuching, Sarawak
telephone : +60.82.411 066
facsimile : +60.82.411 066
nelsontangallery@yahoo.com
nelsontangallery.com

Penang Museum
Ground Floor, Dewan Sri Pinang
Lebuh Farquhar (Light Street)
George Town, 10200 Penang
telephone : +60.4.261 3144
facsimile : +60.4.261 4544
muzium@po.jaring.my
www.penangmuseum.com

Pucuk Rebung Museum Gallery
302A Ampang Mall, Suria KLCC
Kuala Lumpur City Centre
50088 Kuala Lumpur
telephone : +60.3.2382 0769
facsimile : +60.3.2382 1108

Sabah Museum
telephone : +60.88.253 199
facsimile : +60.88.240 230
www.mzm.sabah.gov.my

Shah Alam Gallery
Persiaran Tasik
40000 Shah Alam, Selangor
telephone : +60.3.5510 5334
facsimile : +60.3.5510 2081
enquiry@galerishahalam.org.my
www.galerishahalam.org.my

The Actors Studio
T116, 3rd Floor, West Wing, Bangsar
Shopping Centre
285 Jalan Maarof, Bukit Bandaraya
59000 Kuala Lumpur
telephone : +60.3.2094 0400 or
+60.3.2094 1400
facsimile : +60.3.2093 8400
contact@theactorsstudio.com.my
www.theactorsstudio.com.my

SHOPPING

1 Utama Shopping Centre
1 Lebuh Bandar Utama, Bandar
Utama City Centre, Bandar Utama
47800 Petaling Jaya, Selangor
telephone : +60.3.7710 8118
custserv@1utama.com.my

ARTrageously Ramsay Ong Gallery
94 Main Bazaar
93000 Kuching, Sarawak
telephone : +60.82.424 346
facsimile : +60.82.422 926
artrageouslyramsayong@hotmail.com
www.artrageouslyasia.com

Asoka Palaikat
7 Jalan Tuanku Abdul Rahman
PO Box 10649 Kuala Lumpur
telephone : +60.3.2692 7461

Bangsar Shopping Centre
285 Jalan Maarof, Bukit Bandaraya
59000 Kuala Lumpur

Bangsar Village
1 Jalan Telawi Tiga, Bangsar Baru
59100 Kuala Lumpur
telephone : +60.3.2282 1808
facsimile : +60.3.2288 1900

Bangsar Village II
2 Jalan Telawi Satu, Bangsar Baru
59100 Kuala Lumpur
telephone : +60.3.2288 1200

BB Plaza
111 Jalan Bukit Bintang
55100 Kuala Lumpur
telephone : +60.3.2148 7411
facsimile : +60.3.2141 6492
www.udamall.com

Berjaya Times Square
Berjaya Times Square Sdn Bhd
1 Jalan Imbi, 55100 Kuala Lumpur
telephone : +60.3.2144 9821
facsimile : +60.3.2145 2471
general@timessquarekl.com

KL Plaza
179 Jalan Bukit Bintang
55100 Kuala Lumpur
telephone : +60.3.2141 7288

Low Yat Plaza
7 Jalan Bintang, off Jalan Bukit
Bintang, Bukit Bintang Central
55100 Kuala Lumpur
telephone : +60.3.2148 3651
facsimile : +60.3.2148 3664
info@plazalowyat.com
www.plazalowyat.com

Mid Valley Megamall
Mid Valley City Sdn Bhd
22nd Floor, Menara IGB
Mid Valley City, Lingkaran Syed Putra
59200 Kuala Lumpur
telephone : +60.3.2094 8688
facsimile : +60.3.2289 8638 or
+60.3.2289 8628
customerservice@midvalleycity.com
www.midvalley.com.my

Pasir Besar Siti Khadijah
Kota Bahru

Pasar Payang
Jalan Sultan Abidin
Kuala Terengganu

Pavilion Kuala Lump
168 Jalan Bukit Bintang
55100 Kuala Lumpur
telephone : +60.3.2143 8088
www.pavilion-kl.com

Silverfish Books
58–1 Jalan Telawi Tiga, Bangsar Baru
59100 Kuala Lumpur
telephone : +60.3.2284 4837
facsimile : +60.3.2284 4839
info@silverfishbooks.com
www.silverfishbooks.com

S.M. Badjenid + Sons
184 Lebuh Pantai
10300 George Town, Penang
telephone : +60.4.261 0766

Starhill Gallery
181 Jalan Bukit Bintang
55100 Kuala Lumpur
telephone : +60.3.2782 3855
www.starhillgallery.com

Sungei Wang Plaza
99 Jalan Bukit Bintang
55100 Kuala Lumpur
telephone : +60.3.2144 9988
facsimile : +60.3.2144 7788
www.sungeiwang.com

Suria KLCC
Suria KLCC Sdn Bhd
241, 2nd Floor, Suria KLCC
Kuala Lumpur City Centre
50088 Kuala Lumpur
telephone : +60.3.2382 2828
info@suriaklcc.com.my
www.suriaklcc.com.my

Wah Aik
56 Jalan Tokong, Melaka
telephone : +60.6.284 9726

SPAS

Anggun Spa
Hotel Maya
138 Jalan Ampang
50450 Kuala Lumpur
telephone : +60.3.2711 8866
facsimile : +60.3.2711 9966
info@hotelmaya.com.my
www.hotelmaya.com.my

Berjaya Hills Tatami Spa
Colmar Tropicale
KM 48 Persimpangan Bertingkat
Lebuhraya Karak, 28750 Bukit Tinggi
Bentong, Pahang
telephone : +60.9.288 8888
facsimile : +60.9.288 3333
berjayahills@hr.berjaya.com.my
www.berjayaresorts.com/beach
resort_colmar.htm

Body Senses by Mandara
The Pacific Sutera
1 Sutera Harbour Boulevard
88100 Kota Kinabalu, Sabah
telephone : +60.88.318 888
facsimile : +60.88.317 777
malaysia@mandaraspa.com
www.suteraharbour.com

Borneo Spa
Nexus Resort Karambunai
Off Jalan Sepangar Bay
Locked Bag 100
88993 Kota Kinabalu, Sabah
telephone : +60.88.411 222
facsimile : +60.88.411 020
info@nexusresort.com
www.nexusresort.com

CHI, The Spa
Shangri-La's Rasa Sayang Resort + Spa
Batu Feringgi Beach, 11100 Penang
telephone : +60.4.888 8762
facsimile : +60.4.881 1800
rsr@shangri-la.com
www.shangri-la.com

Heavenly Spa
The Westin Langkawi, Resort + Spa
Jalan Pantai Dato Syed Omar
07000 Langkawi, Kedah
telephone : +60.4.960 8888
facsimile : +60.4.966 6414
westin.langkawi@westin.com
www.westinheavenlyspa.starwood
promos.com

Jentayu Spa
11 Jalan Gelenggang
Bukit Damansara
50490 Kuala Lumpur
telephone : +60.3.2094 4428
enquiries@jentayuspa.com.my

JivaRhu
Tanjung Rhu Resort
Mukim Ayer Hangat
07000 Langkawi, Kedah
telephone : +60.4.959 1033
facsimile : +60.4.959 1899
resort@tanjungrhu.com.my
www.jivarhu.com.my

Mandara Spa
Prince Hotel + Residence
Jalan Conlay, 50450 Kuala Lumpur
telephone : +60.3.2170 8777
facsimile : +60.3.2170 8776
malaysia@mandaraspa.com
www.princehotelkl.com.my

The Magellan Sutera
1 Sutera Harbour Boulevard
88100 Kota Kinabalu, Sabah
telephone : +60.88.318 888
facsimile : +60.88.317 777
malaysia@mandaraspa.com

Miri Marriott Resort + Spa
Jalan Temenggong Datuk
Oyong Lawai
98000 Miri, Sarawak
telephone : +60.85.421 121 ext 7555
facsimile : +60.85.402 855
www.marriott.com

Martha Tilaar Spa Spa Eastern
Rejuvenating Centre
18th Floor, Crown Princess Hotel
182 Jalan Tun Razak
50400 Kuala Lumpur
telephone : +60.3.2775 3868

Ozmosis
1st Floor, 16 Jalan Telawi Dua
Bangsar Baru
59100 Kuala Lumpur
telephone : +60.3.2287 0380
facsimile : +60.3.2287 6318
www.ozmosis.com.my

Senjakala Urban Spa
20 Jalan Pudu Lama
50200 Kuala Lumpur
telephone : +60.3.2031 8082
info@senjakala.com
www.senjakala.com

Spa Indrani
S27 Pamper Floor, Starhill Gallery
181 Jalan Bukit Bintang
50450 Kuala Lumpur
telephone : +60.3.2782 3868
facsimile : +60.3.2782 3867
www.spaindrani.com

Spa Village
Cameron Highlands Resort
39000 Tanah Rata
Cameron Highlands, Pahang
telephone : +60.5.491 1100
facsimile : +60.5.491 1800
www.cameronhighlandsresort.com

The Majestic Malacca
188 Jalan Bunga Raya, 75100 Melaka
telephone : +60.6.289 8000
facsimile : +60.6.289 8080
mmh@ytlhotels.com.my
www.majesticmalacca.com/spa-
village/index.htm

The Spa at the Four Seasons Resort Langkawi
Jalan Tanjung Rhu, 07000 Langkawi
Kedah Darul Aman, Malaysia
telephone : +60.4.950 8888
facsimile : +60.4.950 8899
reservations.lan@fourseasons.com
www.fourseasons.com/langkawi

The Spa at The Andaman Langkawi
Jalan Teluk Datai, PO Box 94
07000 Langkawi
Kedah Darul Aman, Malaysia
telephone : +60.4.959.1088
facsimile : +60.4.959 1168
andaman@ghmhotels.com
www.theandaman.com

The Spa at The Datai Langkawi
Jalan Teluk Datai, 07000 Langkawi
Kedah Darul Aman, Malaysia
telephone : +60.4.959 2500
facsimile : +60.4.959 2600
datai@ghmhotels.com
www.langkawi-resorts.com/dataik